MERCY

BECOMING A PERSON OF COMPASSION, ACCEPTANCE, & FORGIVENESS

C. SAMUEL STORMS

FOREWORD BY
JONI EARECKSON TADA

NAVPRESS
A MINISTRY OF THE NAVIGATORS
P.O. BOX 6000, COLORADO SPRINGS, COLORADO 80934

The Navigators is an international Christian organization. Jesus Christ gave His followers the Great Commission to go and make disciples (Matthew 28:19). The aim of The Navigators is to help fulfill that commission by multiplying laborers for Christ in every nation.

NavPress is the publishing ministry of The Navigators. NavPress publications are tools to help Christians grow. Although publications alone cannot make disciples or change lives, they can help believers learn biblical discipleship, and apply what they learn to their lives and ministries.

Library of Congress Catalog Card Number: 91-61391
ISBN 08910-96264

Printed in the United States of America

Contents

To Ann

He has showed you, O man, what is good.
And what does the LORD require of you?
To act justly and TO LOVE MERCY
and to walk humbly with your God.
Micah 6:8

Author

Sam Storms is pastor of Christ Community Church in Ardmore, Oklahoma. After graduating with a degree in history from the University of Oklahoma, Sam earned his Th.M. from Dallas Theological Seminary and his Ph.D. from the University of Texas at Dallas.

To Love Mercy is Sam's sixth book. Among his published works are *Healing & Holiness, Reaching God's Ear, Chosen for Life,* and *The Grandeur of God,* as well as numerous articles.

Sam and his wife, Ann, live with their two daughters, Melanie and Joanna, in Ardmore.

Foreword

I was sitting by my friend's coffee table, wrestling with whether or not I should tell her about the depression that had gripped me for several days. I decided to open up.

Did she have time to listen, I asked?

"Sure," she said, and promptly rose to retrieve a whistling teakettle from the stove. As she poured, I took a deep breath and started to unfold my problem.

Pause. "Milk in your tea?" Nod yes. Start again. Phone rings. "Wait a minute." Pick up where we left off. Knock at the door. "What were you saying?" More distractions. Friend half-listens. Friend gets up to warm tea.

Help. I hurt.

Here is misery that needs mercy, a burden that needs bearing. And I'm not the only one to whom this happens. In fact, I probably do the same to others who hurt—more often than I realize.

"People matter." Sam Storms writes those words as though God Himself said them . . . and it breaks my heart. Sam writes more: "Beneath the water-line of every life are the frustrated longings, sinful schemes, thoughts, and fantasies of a fallen soul . . . here are where people are hurting. Tragically, we rarely encounter one another at that level. . . . How adept we have become in the ability to get along without one another."

People matter. They matter most to God.

That's why they should matter to us. Instinctively we know that. But being the Lord's hands and heart to those who hurt . . . demands. And, we think, it demands so much. Perhaps that's why we cringe at the misery that needs mercy, we shun the burden that requires bearing. So much easier, it is, to point a hurting friend to a cross-stitched verse set behind glass in a pretty frame. It's the polite, safe thing to do—rather than help our friend live that scripture, love it, fight it, breathe it, make it their own.

It matters how we love, Sam reminds us.

All our lives we've heard that Christ is our sufficiency. Jesus is enough. The Lord is our all. Yes, thank God, it's true! But we dare not wad up those truths into trite platitudes to be tossed at one another, while we stand at a respectable arms-length distance.

"Christ is our sufficiency" should glow with the warm heart-beat of love that is as real as flesh and blood. "Jesus is enough" should be words spoken straight ahead with a smile that involves, that invites. "The Lord is our all" should be the covering with which we gently enfold a hurting friend.

To Love Mercy will help you become the person of compassion, acceptance, and forgiveness you know you must be.

It matters that much.

—Joni Eareckson Tada

Preface

This book would probably never have been written were it not for the ministry of Dr. Lawrence J. Crabb, Jr. The Holy Spirit used Dr. Crabb to effect a profound spiritual transformation in my life and perspective as a pastor. This book is an attempt to share with others what has happened to me as a result.

One of my deepest concerns as a pastor is the failure of Christians to minister to one another in the local church. Too often people simply assume that only "the minister" is supposed to minister. *To Love Mercy* is intended to be a direct and frontal assault on that horribly unbiblical notion.

That doesn't mean I intend to be negative. On the contrary, my goal is a positive and constructive attempt to equip the saints for the work of ministry (Ephesians 4:11-13). My prayer is that what I say will provide you not only the incentive but also the practical tools to heal the brokenhearted, encourage the downcast, and instruct the ill-informed.

The counseling model of Larry Crabb serves as the framework within which this is done. His analysis of why Christians have problems and how biblical solutions may be found is the driving force behind much of what I have written.

But please don't hold Dr. Crabb accountable for my mistakes! There may be places where I have either misinterpreted or misapplied his concepts. There may also be ideas developed in this book with which he would disagree. In brief, I alone am to be blamed for the shortcomings of this book.

A special word of acknowledgment is due the elders of Christ Community Church in Ardmore, Oklahoma. I can't imagine what I would have done without their encouragement and support.

I would also like to thank Steve Webb of NavPress. His encouragement and editorial skills contributed immeasurably to the completion of this book.

As usual, my wife, Ann, has been of immeasurable help. She knew long before I did that this book needed to be written. She knew that *I* needed to write it. To her it is affectionately dedicated.

One more thing. All the people in this book are real. Their stories are true. However, the names have been changed and the circumstances sufficiently altered to protect their privacy and identity.

ONE

A Pastor's Personal Confession

What you are about to read is a confession of error. It is an admission of how wrong I've been: wrong about myself; wrong about other people; wrong about the way God has called me to serve them.

I enjoy being right. There's nothing quite like the thrill of knowing that I know what I'm talking about. The only thing that comes close is knowing that *others* know that I know what I'm talking about!

Does that sound arrogant to you? My guess is it does. Worse than arrogant, that attitude is pompous and prideful. In a word, it is sin. So why am I bringing it up? Because it helps to explain why I've had such a difficult time writing this opening chapter.

My pride makes this very painful. I've rewritten these opening paragraphs at least a dozen times, hoping to find an alternative way of making the same point. My soul even now is screaming, "Don't do it!" Something inside me says, "Keep your guard up. . . . There is safety in silence. . . . There's security in the status quo. . . . Dirty laundry should stay hidden in the hamper, not hung out on the pages of a book!"

No, I haven't committed either adultery or murder. My sin was far more subtle, but not for that reason any less destructive. In fact, I had learned to disguise my sin to look like righteousness. Let me explain.

PROTECTED BY A PULPIT

In the earlier years of my ministry, I maintained that personal needs were better left unspoken. If you had a problem, the Holy Spirit was more than capable of handling it without getting other people involved. My opinion of those who insisted on talking about their struggles was not very high. Those who actually sought counsel ranked even lower. Wasn't the Bible enough? These people didn't need *me*. They needed my *teaching*. As I look back, it grieves me to think how many people may have avoided seeking my help, or thought I was too busy reading books to care about their problems.

Those are the men and women who will be most surprised by what I have to say in this book. They probably never dreamed that I would write on this particular subject. To be quite honest, I never dreamed of it either. After all, my interests at the time were of a decidedly academic nature. Being a scholar was valued more than being a servant (which isn't to say you shouldn't be both).

I always felt more comfortable in a library or classroom than in a counseling office or the living room of someone's home. It was easier, and a lot less threatening, to debate the proper mode of baptism than to get entangled in someone's emotional and spiritual struggles. I always thought it better (and less complicated!) to discuss the millennium than delve into the feelings of rejection and inferiority and resentment that plague so many Christians.

I still enjoy reading the Bible and books about the Bible. If anything, my love for the deep things of God has grown and intensified over the years—which I hope is true of you as well. There simply is no substitute for sound doctrine.

But sound doctrine does not by itself produce sanctified disciples. I wish it did. It certainly would make ministry less taxing. The only principal requirement would be to preach well. Just think of it: No time-consuming involvement, no messy details, no heartaches for those whose lives are crumbling like a week-old cookie. If only sound doctrine could do it all! But it can't. And God doesn't want it to.

Let me explain that statement. I'm not waffling on the power of God's truth. For years I have been trying my best to preach sound doctrine, and I fully intend to continue doing so. But regrettably, and to my shame, I preached and proclaimed and expounded and explained, all the time assuming that nothing more was necessary. My task as a minister, so I thought, was to analyze the Bible, announce my findings to the people, and then let the Holy Spirit apply it to their lives. To go beyond that was to risk trespassing on God's territory. I certainly didn't want to be guilty of presuming to do what only the Holy Spirit can accomplish.

Since I believed in the sufficiency of Scripture (and still do!), I thought it unnecessary, perhaps even unwise, to become too closely involved in the struggles of the people I ministered to. My calling was to teach them, not meddle in their personal affairs. Given enough time and enough exegetical insights, they were bound to emerge as mature, godly Christians. At least that's what I thought.

And of course some of them did, by God's grace. But I am persuaded that such people are probably in the minority. *Far too many Christians in our evangelical churches are top-heavy: heads full of sound doctrine but hearts that ache from emptiness.* When first I recognized this problem, the solution seemed simple enough: Just fill their heads with even *more* sound doctrine and pray that the Holy Spirit would make it trickle down!

Am I suggesting, then, that we stop preaching doctrine and reduce the time we spend in Bible study? God forbid! What, then, *should* we do? Let me begin sketching an answer to that question by making a confession.

For years my dedication to the careful exposition of Holy Scripture and the maintenance of theological orthodoxy was motivated by more than just a belief in the sufficiency of the Bible. I don't pretend to speak for anyone except myself, but I am compelled to admit that my pulpit ministry was often fueled by more than mere theological conviction. I could never quite put my finger on it before reading something Larry Crabb says in his book *Inside Out*:

> Perhaps it's time to screw up our courage and attack the sacred cow: We must admit that simply knowing the contents of the Bible is not a sure route to spiritual growth. There is an awful assumption in evangelical circles that if

> we can just get the Word of God into people's heads, then the Spirit of God will apply it to their hearts. That assumption is awful, not because the Spirit never does what the assumption supposes, but because it has excused pastors and leaders from the responsibility to tangle with people's lives. Many remain safely hidden behind pulpits, hopelessly out of touch with the struggles of their congregations, proclaiming the Scriptures with a pompous accuracy that touches no one. Pulpits should provide bridges, not barriers, to life-changing relationships.[1]

"Excused from the responsibility to tangle with people's lives." Ouch! You have no way of knowing how painful it is for me to read those words, even today. When I first thought about what Crabb was saying, my immediate response was one of self-defense. "Maybe other pastors," I said, "but not *me*!" But the Holy Spirit refused to let me off so easily. My only hope for peace of mind was to face some disturbing questions and answer them honestly.

Could it really be that my philosophy of preaching had been at least partly shaped by self-interest? Certainly I believed then and still do that all Scripture is "God-breathed," and because it is God-breathed is "useful for teaching, rebuking, correcting and training in righteousness, so that the man of God may be thoroughly equipped for every good work" (2 Timothy 3:16-17).

But had I been using this verse and others such as Hebrews 4:12-13 to justify my personal detachment from people's lives?

At first I was too embarrassed (and too proud) to admit it. Could it possibly be that my insistence on the "sufficiency" of Scripture was a convenient and seemingly biblical way of keeping people and their problems at arm's length? Sadly, the answer is "yes." At the same time I was ministering from a pulpit, I was hiding behind it.

My religious commitment to the centrality of Scripture seemed to provide the perfect excuse for keeping my distance. An otherwise valid theological principle had become a pretext for insulating myself against the pain so many in my congregation were suffering. Intimate involvement with them and the daily turmoil of living in a fallen world was something I wanted to avoid. It was just too time-consuming, too demanding, too agonizing.

Let me see if I can illustrate what this means. Too often we approach the study of the Bible like a high school biology class preparing to dissect a frog. I never had much of a stomach for that sort of thing. I still don't. But with my grade at stake I forced myself to follow instructions.

After making an incision we were told to identify the internal organs of the frog and write a brief explanation of their function. If we had not passed out by then, we turned our attention to a worm or grasshopper and repeated the process. When class was over, we would walk away, leaving the various parts of each animal arranged neatly on the table, ultimately to be swept away and disposed of by the janitor.

We often handle Scripture in a similar way. We dissect the text with scientific accuracy, careful to observe context and setting. We dutifully exegete each passage, applying the principles of interpretation so important to good Bible study. We amass knowledge, perhaps memorize the text, and are generally fascinated by the literary beauty and theological grandeur of God's Word. All of this, of course, is both good and necessary. But too frequently we then just walk away, leaving behind the truths of God's Word like so many body parts from a dead frog.

But in reality *we* are the frogs and God's Word is the surgical knife! It is not so much we who should dissect Scripture as it is Scripture that should be permitted to dissect us. For the Bible is "sharper than any double-edged sword, [and] it penetrates even to dividing soul and spirit, joints and marrow; [and] it judges the thoughts and attitudes of the heart" (Hebrews 4:12).

As we study the Bible, we simply must take what we learn and ask of ourselves some serious, probing questions: What does this text say about God and myself that will enable me to love Him and others more sacrificially? What does this passage say about the way I relate to others and my responsibility to bear their burdens? How can this verse be used to motivate me and others to display the mercy of Christ? In what way does the truth of the text expose my efforts at self-protection and manipulation of others? How am I a different person after having placed my soul under the searchlight of Scripture?

Asking such questions, and answering them honestly, should begin to close the gap between the pulpit and the pew.

A PASSION FOR PEOPLE

Is Scripture any less central in my ministry today? I pray not! It isn't that the Bible is any less important, but that people are *more* important. Not more important than the Bible, just more important *to me* than they were before. I have come to recognize the depths of their pain, their emotional and spiritual struggles, and the ache in their hearts for a meaningful, loving relationship with Jesus Christ and other Christians. I have come to see that if I'm not lovingly and intimately involved in the lives of those who are hurting, all my talk about "love for Christ" is just so much pious speech.

It's amazing how adept we in the twentieth century have become at getting along without each other. We view other people and their problems more as impositions than as opportunities for ministry. Not so Paul. During his confinement in Caesarea he wrote to the Christians in Philippi, "I hope in the Lord Jesus to send Timothy to you soon, that I also may be cheered when I receive news about you" (Philippians 2:19). It was utterly unthinkable to Paul that the believers in Philippi could be in distress while he carried on as if nothing had happened. He longed to be "cheered" by news of their progress, and went so far as to dispatch Timothy to find out as quickly as possible how they were doing.

Paul then had some special things to say about Timothy: "I have no one else like him, who takes a genuine interest in your welfare. For everyone looks out for his own interests, not those of Jesus Christ" (verses 20-21). Paul says he is sending Timothy because this young man, unlike so many others, is genuinely concerned for their welfare.

But notice something else about this last verse. Paul says everyone else "looks out for his own interests, not those of Jesus Christ." Did you catch what he said? I would have expected him to say something like, "everyone else looks out for his own interests, *not yours*." Instead, Paul contrasts concern for the Philippians with lack of concern for *Christ*! Why did he say it that way?

The reason is simple and yet profound. To be concerned for other believers *is* to be concerned for Christ. To lack interest in the things of Christ *is* to lack interest in other Christians. The two are interchangeable and inseparable. That these other people (whoever they may have been) didn't love and care for the Philippians is proof that they didn't love and care for Christ. A true believer displays his devotion to the Savior by his loving concern for and ministry to the saints.

Not long ago a friend of mine was confronted by her pastor with a gentle and no doubt sincere rebuke. "Debbie," he said, "it seems lately that all you talk about is people and their pain. I rarely hear you say anything about the Lord."

I understand where he's coming from. So does Debbie. Jesus must always be at the heart of everything we do. The first and greatest commandment will always be to "love the Lord your God with all your heart and with all your soul and with all your mind" (Matthew 22:37). But there are certainly a lot of ways to express that love, and one of them is by obeying the second greatest commandment: "Love your neighbor as yourself" (verse 39).

Debbie never loved other Christians as an excuse for not loving Christ. Nor was her love for them at any time greater than her love for Christ. Debbie loved other Christians precisely *because* she loved Christ! She carried a burden for their pain because Christ did . . . all the way to the cross.

I'm not suggesting that Debbie's love for other believers is identical with her love for the Savior. I'm simply saying her love for Christians is the *proof* of her love for Christ.

That's why the author of the Epistle to the Hebrews can say, "God is not unjust; he will not forget your work and the love you have shown him as you have helped his people and continue to help them" (Hebrews 6:10). Love for God is revealed in loving, persistent ministry on behalf of God's people. If anything, Debbie's pastor should have said, "How much you must love the Lord, seeing how much you love His children!"

The Apostle John agrees, telling us that "everyone who believes that Jesus is the Christ is born of God, and everyone who loves the father loves his child as well" (1 John 5:1).

There is no choice between loving God or loving His children.

These are not mutually exclusive or separable items. True love for God requires an active, fervent affection for all in His family.

Did Paul love the Lord Jesus Christ? Of course he did! How do you know? Before you list the reasons, let me point to one which, as far as I am concerned, settles it beyond any doubt.

I know Paul loved the Lord Jesus Christ because I know he loved Christians. Take as an example his relationship with the Thessalonians. Listen to how he describes the depth of his feeling for these people: "As apostles of Christ we could have been a burden to you, but we were gentle among you, like a mother caring for her little children. We loved you so much that we were delighted to share with you not only the gospel of God but our lives as well, because you had become so dear to us" (1 Thessalonians 2:6-8).

Sadly, though, Paul had been forced to flee Thessalonica because of opposition to his ministry from both Jews and Gentiles. It was an incredibly grievous experience for him to be cut off from those whom he loved so intensely. The word he uses to express the depths of his pain on being separated from the Thessalonians is *aporphanizo*, translated "torn away" in verse 17. You don't have to be a Greek scholar to know what that means. Paul says, in effect, "We were orphaned! Our agony was no less than that of a parent and child forcibly wrenched from each other's arms!"

A few years ago a young couple in Florida was brought to court and charged with obtaining their adoptive child through illegal measures. The natural mother had filed suit in her attempt to regain legal custody. With tears streaming down his face and his voice cracking under the emotional strain, the judge ruled on behalf of the natural mother. His distress was evoked by the fact that, although the adoptive parents had acted in disregard for the law, there was no mistaking their love for the child.

When the court bailiff took the child from the loving arms of the adoptive father, no words could have described his pain. As I watched this tragic scene on television, I couldn't help but think of Paul's words here in 1 Thessalonians. Bereft of his spiritual children, Paul's heart was breaking. Such tender affection among Christians is in pitifully short supply today. Few of us ever experience such love and unity of faith.

Paul's deep feelings for the Thessalonians is even more remarkable when we consider that, scarcely eight months before he wrote these words, Paul and the Thessalonians hadn't even met! Such deep ties of affection in so short a period of time can be explained only by the power of the gospel.

Nor was Paul's love for the Thessalonians a mere feeling that came and went, never providing tangible proof of its reality. He says, "out of our intense longing we made every effort to see you. For we wanted to come to you—certainly I, Paul, did, again and again—but Satan stopped us" (verses 17-18).

Paul doubled and then redoubled his efforts to return to Thessalonica. It wasn't enough to talk about them or write to them or even pray for them, although he certainly did pray (3:10-13). Paul desperately longed to *see* them, to be *with* them physically, sharing and rejoicing and weeping and worshiping. There is no substitute for fellowship in the physical presence of other Christians. Spending time together in close mutual interaction, sharing needs and voicing words of encouragement, is absolutely indispensable. Christian love may sometimes have to settle for fellowship over the phone, but it is never satisfied until face-to-face intimacy is restored.

Would it surprise you to discover that even Satan knows how critical Christian fellowship is for the life of the individual and the well-being of the Church? That's one reason why he personally intervened to make it physically impossible for Paul to return to Thessalonica (2:18). Paul was left disconsolate, bereft of his beloved fellow-believers. But only "in person," he says, "not in thought" (2:17). Out of sight, yes, but by no means out of mind. There was a bond between them that no mere geographical distance could break. Satan could not destroy their mutual affection.

With his options greatly reduced, and his heart heavily burdened, Paul sent Timothy to Thessalonica (3:1-5). And when Timothy returned to Paul with news of how well the Thessalonians were doing, he could barely restrain himself:

> But Timothy has just now come to us from you and has brought good news about your faith and love. He has told us that you always have pleasant memories of us and that you long to see us, just as we also long to see you.

> Therefore, brothers, in all our distress and persecution we were encouraged about you because of your faith. For now we really live, since you are standing firm in the Lord. How can we thank God enough for you in return for all the joy we have in the presence of our God because of you? Night and day we pray most earnestly that we may see you again and supply what is lacking in your faith. (3:6-10)

The word translated "brought good news" in verse 6 is the one used frequently in the New Testament for preaching the gospel. Again we see how close Paul and the Thessalonians had become, for he declares that news of their perseverance and progress was a veritable "gospel" to his soul!

"The feeling is mutual," the Thessalonians told Timothy. Paul's desire to see them is matched only by their desire to see him! What a remarkable relationship these believers had. Their joy, their very lives, were wrapped up in one another. It is as if Paul never had really lived until now, now that he has heard of their stand for Christ. "I was lifeless," says the apostle, "a dead weight oppressed and disheartened me, until I heard about you!" What more can I do, he seems to say, but return to my knees in prayer, night and day, beseeching God that I might once again see your face?

How would you describe your relationship with other Christians? Would you use the words of Paul? Can you honestly say that your love for others in the Body of Christ is like the love that bonded Paul and the Thessalonians? Are you eager to see their faces, dejected and inconsolable when separated? So often our approach to so-called "Christian living" is to enter church quietly and unobtrusively, get our religious time-card punched, and *then hurriedly retreat behind the safe walls of our homes*. Too much contact with others, too much communication might lead to entanglements that we so desperately want to avoid.

How tragic! Oh, that we might love and long for one another as Paul did for the Thessalonians and they for him. Oh, that God might touch our hearts that we in turn might touch others. It may sound trite, but *people matter*. Who can doubt that they mattered to Paul, perhaps the greatest advocate of the sufficiency of Scripture who ever lived? If Paul spent time in the "ivory tower" of theological reflection, it was not only to expand his own mind but also to prepare himself for wrestling with the daily trials of his people. For Paul, truth was not an end in itself, but a divinely ordained tool for building Christlike character.

Like the Apostle Paul, Derek and I had always loved the truth. We spent much of our time together discussing the meaning of some obscure passage, or if a new book had interpreted it correctly. We were at home in our own "ivory tower," two friends who sharpened their theological teeth chewing on the meat of God's Word. But I never knew what it meant to be Derek's brother in Christ until a memorable Sunday night.

The service was about to begin when Derek grabbed my arm and led me into the church kitchen. I knew immediately something was wrong. His voice quivered, his eyes were moist. He fought hard to get the words out. He was uncertain of how I'd react.

"Sally is seeing another man!" Not a whole lot more was said. I'd known Derek and Sally for a long time. I'd heard their testimonies. I counted them among my closest friends. I was stunned.

I never told Derek this, but when he broke the news to me that Sunday evening there suddenly came to mind Paul's words in 1 Corinthians 12:26, "If one part [of the Body of Christ] suffers, every part suffers with it." I had preached what I thought at the time was a powerful sermon on that passage. But it never really clicked until that evening as Derek's pain became my own.

Rejoicing with those who rejoice is one thing. But to "mourn with those who mourn" (Romans 12:15) was something I had consistently avoided until now. But no more. Here was misery needing mercy. Here was a burden that needed bearing. Without speaking, almost spontaneously, we embraced.

Without speaking, almost spontaneously, we embraced. There we were, two grown men hugging in the church kitchen with tears streaming down our faces! If I say I'm glad no one saw us, it shows how fearful I was of letting down my guard. What Derek needed, then and there, was someone who cared enough about his pain that nothing else mattered.

It has been several years now since Derek first shared his pain with me. I'd like to say it all turned out okay . . . but it didn't. I suffered with Derek and Sally through a painful separation and divorce. Both were wounded. Both bear deep scars. Derek and I are closer now than ever. That's because when the pain is unbearable and the guilt piles high and all the explanations in the world no longer make sense, there is this unshakeable reality: One Christian loving another Christian with the love of Christ.

Paul and the Thessalonians had something quite special. Derek and I think we know what it was. But we want more. My guess is you do too. So how do we get it?

Among other things, we must learn how to bear the burdens threatening the spiritual and emotional growth of our brothers and sisters in the Body of Christ. The problems and perplexities and struggles of the person in the pew next to you must somehow become your own. It means that each of us must serve and sacrifice and sympathize with those who are hurting. As Larry Crabb expressed it, we must be willing "to tangle with people's lives." We must learn *to love mercy*.

I began this chapter by making a painful confession of my own failure in this area. Whereas I had succeeded well enough in teaching people, I had rarely touched them with the compassion and sensitivity so essential to authentic Christian ministry. I hope it wasn't from lack of love, though who among us has ever loved as fully as we should? I suspect it was due primarily to a strange mixture of ignorance and fear.

There were times when I simply didn't know how to deal with people's crippling problems. I was baffled by human behavior and the underlying motivation for it. Whenever I heard pleas for help, I felt spiritually paralyzed. And on those rare occasions when I did understand the dynamics of people's problems, I was too afraid of the sacrifices closer involvement in their lives would entail. The risks were just more than I was willing to take.

God continues to deal with me in this matter. It isn't always easy. At times I'm a little reluctant. But His grace always prevails. He has set me on a new path, one that I pray will result in tender mercy on my part, a glad and effective bearing of the burdens others are facing. This book is the first step down that path. Like the Apostle Paul before us, like Debbie, Derek, and so many others, will you walk it with me?

TWO

Barriers to Burden-Bearing

On Sunday mornings as I prepare to address the people in my congregation, I often find myself asking the question: "Who's next?" Who among these seemingly content and Christlike men and women will be the next to fall? In view of recent scandals among the clergy, they are probably looking back at me and asking the same question!

I realize how cynical and pessimistic that sounds. Believe me, the last thing I want to do is undermine anyone's faith in the power of God's grace to transform lives and relationships. I have seen many examples of the Holy Spirit rescuing and restoring people in what otherwise would be hopeless situations.

But if cynicism is one extreme to avoid, naïveté is the other. Hurting hearts are everywhere, crying out for relief, seeking mercy. The reason we don't hear those cries as often as we should is that usually they are deliberately muffled. We Christians are incredibly skilled at camouflaging our inner struggles. We have a remarkable knack for convincing others we are on top of the world when we're really in the pits.

I see it in people all the time. Outwardly they appear to be fine. They don't lead scandalous lives. They don't use profanity. They observe good hygiene. They diligently pay their taxes and their tithe. They faithfully attend church, sing hymns (often from memory), and speak intelligently whenever a theological argument erupts. They know the rules of the game and tend to abide by them. They give generously of their time and talents to support the work of the church. What more could anyone want?

Don't get me wrong. I certainly do not wish it were otherwise. Who wants a scandal, or empty pews—or worse yet, empty offering plates! But is that what being a Christian is all about? Is it simply a matter of crossing our theological t's and dotting our public i's? Perhaps that's enough if one wants to be a Pharisee. But real Christian holiness is more than skin-deep. It is more than merely maintaining a respectable public image and cogently defending the deity of Christ.

THE HURTS PEOPLE HIDE

What I'm driving at is this: People are hurting, appearances notwithstanding. *Christian* people are hurting. We are struggling with doubts, fears, crippling anxiety, thoughts of suicide, immoral fantasies, resentment, bitterness, depression, fractured relationships, feelings of isolation, and envy.

Ours is not a large church, but I confront these problems every day. The struggles in our body are all too real, and although most of us manage a smile on Sunday morning, I know how deeply many are hurting, for I've been there myself all too often.

One Sunday morning I spent some extra time just scanning the faces of the crowd before me. I knew that for many in the audience it wasn't easy being there. My eyes first fell on one woman whose father had recently died. It had been sudden and unsettling. No sooner had she dealt with the grief of losing him than her sister, a mother of three young children, was diagnosed with cancer. Her death still puzzles us all.

Then I noticed a man who has long suffered from a serious eye problem. Both surgery and the ever-present threat of blindness have weighed heavily on him. Then I saw a dear lady whose stamina astounds me. A victim of her husband's infidelity, she was left emotionally devastated, financially strapped, and solely responsible for raising two teenagers. Her job demands that she travel extensively, adding to the burden she already must bear.

I can't even count the number who come each Sunday distraught over unsaved loved ones. Not a week passes without one precious lady requesting prayer for her brother. His rejection of the gospel tears at her daily. Another's father is a Mormon. Another's husband simply couldn't care less.

One couple in particular continues to amaze me. They have survived an incredible ordeal, but not without scars to show for it. The husband was recently released from prison. He refused to plead guilty to the charges against him, vigorously maintaining his innocence. They lost a business that had taken a lifetime to build, as well as their home and untold thousands of dollars in legal fees and fines. The emotional strain has taken its physical toll as well, as he now faces each day uncertain if his severely damaged heart will sustain him. They've come through it all surprisingly well, but it's hard for them not to be bitter.

There are so many others. My soul aches for the young man whose wife left him, for the couple with serious marital and monetary problems, for the church leader whose father is stricken with Alzheimer's disease, and for the young mother whose husband just died of leukemia at the age of twenty-eight, only eight months after the birth of his first child.

Not long ago I officiated at the funeral of a remarkable Christian woman whose entire life had been dedicated to the cause of Christ. It wasn't easy watching her husband struggle to face each day without her, with whom he had shared almost fifty years of his life. I can't remember a conversation with him that didn't concern her. He once said that when the Lord made them "one flesh" in marriage He must have used "super-glue"! When death tore them apart, he died too. Six months later I was preaching another funeral.

And then there is the young woman whose nephew became a paraplegic following a tragic car accident. She has questions that can't be answered with a simple phrase or a well-worn verse . . . not if we want to show her the kind of mercy our Lord would have shown.

I don't think our church is any different from most. These are hard-working, God-fearing evangelical Christians. And a lot of them are crying inside. Some are not afraid to cry outside as well. Depression, self-doubt, fear, loneliness, shattered dreams, disillusionment, business failures, all take their toll. And God calls on you and me to bear their burdens.

THE PAIN OF A PSALMIST

When I see people whose pain I also feel, my mind goes back to the psalms, to a somewhat obscure man by the name of Heman. He was the father of seventeen children and one of the choir directors appointed by David to lead the congregation of Israel in praise and worship (1 Chronicles 6:31-33, 15:16-17, 16:41-42, 25:5-7).

Heman was both a singer and a musician. Some people claim that musicians are especially prone to radical mood swings. That may not be altogether fair, but it certainly applies to the man who authored Psalm 88.

This hymn of personal woe has been called the darkest, most despondent, and saddest of all the psalms. Unlike the other psalms of lament, this one does not conclude with praise or a declaration of joy and confidence in God. Heman is as troubled at the close as he was at the beginning. His anguish is unrelenting. His distress is unrelieved. Aside from the opening verse there is no word of hope, no consolation for his soul:[1]

> O LORD, the God who saves me,
> day and night I cry out before you.
> May my prayer come before you;
> turn your ear to my cry. (verses 1-2)

In the midst of his doubts and despair, Heman still knows he is saved. And he knows it is God who has saved him. But beyond that he is unsure. His prayers go unanswered, so it seems. His cry for help falls on deaf ears:

> For my soul is full of trouble
> and my life draws near the grave.
> I am counted among those who go down to the pit;
> I am like a man without strength.
> I am set apart with the dead,
> like the slain who lie in the grave,
> whom you remember no more,
> who are cut off from your care.

You have put me in the lowest pit,
in the darkest depths.
Your wrath lies heavily upon me;
you have overwhelmed me with all your waves.
(verses 3-7)

Like a jar brim-full of bitter water, Heman's soul overflows with trouble. He might as well be dead, for his life seems to be hardly worth living:

You have taken from me my closest friends
and have made me repulsive to them. (verse 8)

Perhaps Heman suffered from a disease or affliction that made his physical appearance loathsome to the sight (cf. Job 2:11-13, 17:7). Or it may simply be that his so-called friends could take it no more. Sadly, it doesn't take much of an excuse for us to justify abandoning our friends when they become an imposition on our lives. No one enjoys spending too much time with a Job. Perhaps Heman's trials finally became more than they were willing to bear. So they left him to his misery:

I am confined and cannot escape;
my eyes are dim with grief.

I call to you, O LORD, every day;
I spread out my hands to you.
Do you show your wonders to the dead?
Do those who are dead rise up and praise you?
Is your love declared in the grave,
your faithfulness in Destruction?
Are your wonders known in the place of darkness,
or your righteous deeds in the land of oblivion?
(verses 8-12)

Heman is persistent in his prayers, but his patience is wearing thin. We don't know how much Old Testament saints knew about the after-life, but Heman sees no profit for God should he die. "I can't praise you from the grave," he cries. "What good am I to you if these troubles end my life?"

> But I cry to you for help, O LORD;
> in the morning my prayer comes before you.
> Why, O LORD, do you reject me
> and hide your face from me?
>
> From my youth I have been afflicted and close to death;
> I have suffered your terrors and am in despair.
> Your wrath has swept over me;
> your terrors have destroyed me.
> All day long they surround me like a flood;
> they have completely engulfed me. (verses 13-17)

Like a lot of us, Heman can't help but interpret his distress as a sign that maybe God has abandoned him. After all, it isn't as if he has suffered only for a while. Don't we all? No, Heman has seen hardship from his youth on. His agony is life-long:

> You have taken my companions and loved ones from me;
> the darkness is my closest friend. (verse 18)

Bereft of friends, cut off from the compassion and love of his family, Heman has but one companion to soothe his pains: darkness. Alone, isolated, seemingly without hope, he feels engulfed by night. How tragic! As commentator Franz Delitzsch has said, "the gloom of melancholy does not brighten up to become a hope, the Psalm dies away in Job-like lamentation."[2]

I am not at all suggesting that Heman's experience is normative. There is joy in Christ. There is deliverance in God's grace. Still we should not write him off as some sort of demented exception to an otherwise universal rule. *Heman's experience is not as uncommon as we might think.* There are people all around us, even sitting in the church pew at our side, who know and feel all too well the sorrows of Heman. They are not surprised by Psalm 88. They read it and nod with understanding, and weep. Like Heman, darkness is the closest friend they have.

But unlike Heman, few people today want their problems

aired in public, especially when everyone else *seems* to be doing so well. So we hide our inner ache from view. We learn how to dress for success and smile on cue. We touch all the theological bases, avoid all the moral taboos, and become adept in responding well to the question, "Hi! How're ya' doin'?"

Our reluctance to share our burdens with others would shock the saints of old. As I read the psalms of David, Asaph, Heman, and others, I see nothing of our modern fear of exposure. The psalmists candidly declare their distress (Psalm 4:1), sorrow (6:7), loneliness (25:16, 142:4), affliction (25:16), grief (35:14), mourning (35:14), fear (55:5), and dismay (143:4). They don't hesitate to confess that they are consumed by anguish (31:10), weak with sorrow (31:9, 119:28), worn out from groaning (6:6), bowed down and brought low (38:6), feeble and utterly crushed (38:8), troubled by sin (38:18), downcast (42:5-6), forlorn (35:12), faint (6:2), overcome by trouble (116:3), and in desperate need (79:8).

Yes, the psalms are also replete with praise, jubilation, and joy. But perhaps this is in part due to their readiness to deal openly with the anguish in their souls. It is only when we confess and confront the pain in our hearts that the fullness of Christ's consolation, mediated through the merciful ministry of others, can do its work in our lives.

LOOKING ON THE INSIDE

There is simply no escape from the desperate need to address with honesty and forthrightness the agony on the inside. Perhaps an illustration will help. When the Titanic set sail on its maiden voyage from England to New York City, no one could have anticipated the impending disaster. On the night of April 14, 1912, the British steamer struck an iceberg, ripping a 300-foot gash in its hull. We all know the tragic aftermath.

Viewed from above the water's surface, the iceberg seemed to present little cause for alarm. But the danger lurked beneath the surface, hidden from view in the dark waters of the Atlantic.

People are a lot like that. It's easy to see how they dress, to hear the way they talk, to observe their manners. If the measure of spiritual maturity were nothing more than what we see on the outside, we would have good reason to feel confident about the state of the Church. After all, most Christians seem to lead respectable lives. They rarely indulge—at least not publicly—in those forms of excess that we typically call sin. We assume they have made great progress in the Christian life. So we ask them to teach Sunday school, elect them to serve on the church board, and join with them in singing, "It is well with my soul."

But is it really? Is it *really* well with our souls? That's virtually impossible to know without becoming personally and intimately involved in another individual's life. And few of us are willing to do that. We see each other week after week in the hallways of the church building, are courteous in our acknowledgment of each other, and perhaps join together in drinking a quick cup of coffee between Sunday school and the worship service.

This sort of cordial but superficial conversation, which so often passes for "Christian fellowship" in our churches, will never touch people where they live. It may tell us what is going on above the water line, but little more.

What I am seeing more and more is the externally well-groomed Christian who is dying inside. He or she is often motivated to acts of visible "holiness" more by self-protection—that urge we spoke of earlier to refuse to expose our pain—than by wanting to glorify Christ and love others

That is why we often find the Word of God so threatening; it refuses to stop where we do: "It penetrates even to dividing soul and spirit, joints and marrow; it judges the thoughts and attitudes of the heart" (Hebrews 4:12).

There it is: The thoughts and attitudes of the heart! Beneath the water line of every life are the urges, motives, thoughts, fantasies, frustrated longings, crippling doubts and sinful schemes of a fallen soul. This is where people are hurting.

Tragically, though, we rarely encounter one another at such depth. There must be a reason for our reluctance to relate and minister to one another where it is most desperately needed. What accounts for the hesitation and fear that undermines the possibility of our experiencing authentic, effective Christian fellowship?

One reason is the silent assumption that people who are hurting and share their secret struggles with others are weak and immature. Call it rugged individualism or whatever you wish, the fact remains that among evangelicals maturity is often identified with a form of "spiritual stoicism." The result is often that people are intimidated into silence, not wanting to appear "sub-Christian." Let me explain what I mean.

In March of 1988, I attended the Institute for Biblical Counseling in Dallas, Texas, a week-long seminar led by Dr. Larry Crabb and Dr. Dan Allender. On the second day I ran into a former classmate from seminary. We hadn't seen each other in more than ten years. As he extended his hand he smiled, and with a look of surprise at seeing me there, said: "Sam! What's a good Calvinist like you doing at a seminar like this?"

Although he quickly assured me that he was only kidding, the question was not altogether inappropriate. I *am* a Calvinist. In fact, I have written a book defending the Calvinistic doctrine of unconditional election.[3] It saddens me to say this, but many Calvinists are thought by other evangelical Christians to be cold, detached, and somewhat impersonal. To my everlasting shame I myself have probably contributed a little to that image. Calvinists are generally known for their theological orthodoxy, particularly as it relates to the doctrine of divine sovereignty. For that I am grateful. But we are also sometimes known for a conspicuous lack of pastoral sensitivity.

For reasons I do not fully understand, Calvinists and other Christians who place great emphasis on theological precision do not always display a corresponding and equally fervent love for people. Perhaps they feel that, were they to do so, they would risk being accused of "going soft" on the sovereignty of God and the sufficiency of Scripture. But nothing in Scripture would lead us to believe that a commitment to bearing one another's burdens is incompatible with a zeal for doctrinal integrity. And I was at the seminar to learn more about bearing those burdens, about loving mercy.

BEARING ONE ANOTHER'S BURDENS

Paul states it simply and to the point: "Bear one another's burdens, and thus fulfill the law of Christ" (Galatians 6:2, NASB). Paul doesn't mean "tolerate" the burdens and weaknesses of others. The word *bear* does not suggest that our duty is to endure or put up with the problems other Christians experience. The *New International Version* renders this verb as "carry." We are to take the oppressive emotional and spiritual weight off other people's souls by shifting it to ourselves.

Paul's exhortation is apparently based on two assumptions: First, we all have burdens; second, God does not intend for us to bear them alone. Neither of these assumptions, however, has gone unchallenged.

Some would have us believe that only a minority of Christians experience the sort of burdens Paul has in mind. They surely reach this conclusion by failing to consider what is happening below the water line in the lives of most Christians. If our assessment of someone's spiritual condition is based solely on how they behave within the protective walls of a church sanctuary, we will think of them as relatively burden-free. But there is obviously more to Christian character than reverent behavior on Sunday.

Most of us would be shocked if we really knew how many personal worlds were breaking down under the burdens of sin. After his own world collapsed under the weight of infidelity, Gordon MacDonald made this very discovery. In his excellent book *Rebuilding Your Broken World*, he refers to a number of "broken-world myths," such as the myth that,

> *broken worlds are the exception, not the rule*. They are merely anomalies in life, and the less we think about them the better. Broken worlds never happen to good people; only phonies, rebels, and those less than smart really go through broken-world moments. Furthermore, to spend too much time brooding on the possibility of broken-world experiences is to invite the event. It's better to think only happy, positive thoughts.[4]

As I said before, we don't want to admit that this is really a myth, lest we be forced to devote more time and effort than we are willing to give in helping people rebuild their shattered lives. We are easily deceived by the myth that only a few people labor under such burdens—because most people hide it so well. MacDonald refers to these people as members of "the society of secret carriers." They had been there all along. He simply hadn't known how many there were until his own burden became too heavy to bear alone. He writes,

> I had been a pastor for more than twenty-five years, and during that time I'd probably come into contact with literally tens of thousands of people. Although I was always aware that congregations were full of men and women who were living with self-inflicted or other-inflicted wounds, I never (never, never, never) had any idea of how many more secret carriers there really were and how deep were their shame and their pain.[5]

It would be so convenient and sanitary for us to ignore this fact. But souls are at stake. As MacDonald says, we simply cannot turn our backs on,

> those numberless people who walk into sanctuaries all over the world carrying their secrets behind bright clothing and forced smiles. They sing the songs, pray the prayers, listen to the sermons. And all the while the secrets fester within the private world causing either a constantly broken heart or a hardened heart. They come in fear of their secrets being exposed, and they quite likely go in fear that they will have to live this way for the rest of their lives.[6]

Still others would insist that if people are in fact burdened as badly as I am suggesting, the solution is to entrust them to the care of Christ. After all, didn't the psalmist say, "Cast your cares on the LORD and he will sustain you" (Psalm 55:22)? And what did the Apostle Peter say, but to "cast all your anxiety on him [God] because he cares for you" (1 Peter 5:7)?

Of course Christ cares for us! Paul would be the last person in the world to deny it. The question is not *whether* Christ cares enough to bear the burdens of our hearts, but *how* does He intend to do it? How does He minister to us, comfort us, relieve us of our anxieties and trials? The answer is life-changing: *Christ bears the burdens of your soul in and through other Christians!*

I am reminded of something Paul said in his second letter to the Corinthians. His relationship with these believers had suffered due to the influence of certain false teachers who were seeking to undermine his apostolic authority and to impugn his character. Obviously distressed, Paul had sent Titus to Corinth, hoping thereby to heal the wounds that had been inflicted. Listen to his report of what happened when Titus returned:

> For when we came into Macedonia, this body of ours had no rest, but we were harassed at every turn—conflicts on the outside, fears within. But God, who comforts the downcast, comforted us by the coming of Titus, and not only by his coming but also by the comfort you had given him. He told us about your longing for me, your deep sorrow, your ardent concern for me, so that my joy was greater than ever. (2 Corinthians 7:5-7)

Needless to say, Paul was burdened. He needed the comfort only Christ ultimately can supply. But how did our Lord minister comfort to Paul's heart? He comforted Paul through Titus and the Corinthian Christians! *God* comforted Paul, *God* bore Paul's burden, *God* relieved his distress—*through Titus and the Corinthians!* Divine comfort was provided through human means. God bears our burdens by placing us in vital spiritual union with other believers who desire to bear them for us. In this way the bond of Christian unity and the intimacy of real Christian fellowship are strengthened.

Our duty is inescapably clear. Bear the burdens of others. Unfortunately, though, the prospect of doing that fills a lot of people with absolute terror. Let's face it, personal problems are intimidating. It can be downright frightening when a friend comes to you depressed or bitter or on the verge of divorce. This fear, which so frequently paralyzes our efforts to help, is often born of ignorance. It isn't that we don't want to help; we just don't know *how*.

Most Christians don't understand what is going on beneath

the water line, whether in their own lives or in the lives of others. And a few years ago I would have said, "So what?" I still hear people say that it doesn't really matter what people are doing beneath the surface. All that matters is that they are sinning and need to repent. Well, of course they are sinning; of course they need to repent. But people and their problems are far more complex than that.[7]

Bearing the burdens of others—doing mercy—means we need to know why people have burdens that need bearing! Why do problems develop? What is it about people created in the image of God that leads them to think and feel and act the way they do? What accounts for the way we relate one to another? Why are we so defensive of ourselves? What lies back of our attempts to manipulate the people we profess to love? To put it bluntly: *What makes people tick?*

Until we develop at least a minimal understanding of human nature and human needs, we will be ill-equipped to help those who are hurting. One does not treat cancer with an aspirin, or an upset stomach with penicillin. A wound will only respond to medication appropriately applied. So too with injuries to the soul. For mercy to be effective we must first identify the soul's misery.

In the next chapter I shall explore what motivates you and me at our deepest level of existence. That chapter is without question the most important in the book, for if we do not accurately identify the longings, expectations, fears, and frustrations that lie back of and explain human behavior, our desire to bear the burdens of others will in all likelihood bear little fruit.

THREE

God Made Us Hungry

Bridgett was a petite, blonde eighth-grader who was quite unhappy with her family's decision to move from Allentown, Pennsylvania, to East Greenville. The school guidance counselor thought Bridgett was adjusting well, but her classmates said she had talked about suicide. A week later, she took her stepfather's .22-caliber handgun and shot herself in the head.

The note she left behind was brief, but it spoke volumes: "I shot myself at 5:01 p.m. Do not blame Jim [the stepfather] 'cause he had guns in the house. I love you, Mom. P.S. Everyone at this school hates me."

I read it again. "Everyone at this school hates me." I can't remember ever reading words that touched me as deeply as those. But why? After all, the only thing I knew about Bridgett was what little information appeared in the newspaper article reporting her death.[1] I had almost grown accustomed to reading about teen suicides. What made this one so special? I thought, *Get hold of yourself, Sam! There's nothing you can do about it. After all, it's just a postscript.*

"Everyone at this school hates me."

Why did Bridgett kill herself? She was just thirteen years old. Were there other factors involved that might not have been included in the article? Perhaps. But I think I know why Bridgett took her own life. It's right there in that postscript. Bridgett died of hunger. Her soul starved to death. It staggers us to think that the pain of rejection could become so intense that a young girl would seek relief through death. But that's only because we know so little about the mechanics of the human soul.

Bridgett's final words tell us more than why a thirteen-year-old girl took her own life. Without knowing it, Bridgett gave voice to what is inside of all of us. Bridgett wasn't hungry because she was different. God made us all that way. And the sooner we realize it, the sooner we can begin to enjoy the spiritual supper God's grace has supplied.

A LONGING FOR LOVE

There's a huge billboard along Interstate 35, halfway between Ardmore, Oklahoma, where I live, and Dallas, Texas. It is totally blank except for one statement at the bottom, with an accompanying phone number. It reads: "I want you to want me!"

The point of the message, of course, is that the billboard wants you to want *it*, for the purpose of advertising your product. But to make his point, the owner of the sign has wisely appealed to one of the most basic desires of the human heart: The longing to be loved.

Ask yourself this question: How much happiness will $500 million buy? Few if any of us will ever have opportunity to find out. But Christina Onassis knew. She isn't here to tell us. She died of heart failure in November 1988, at the age of thirty-seven. But I think her answer would have been: "Very, very little."

Christina was the sole heir to her father's massive financial empire. Aristotle Onassis became well-known to Americans when he married Jacqueline Kennedy. Christina knew a little about marriage herself. Four times she went to the altar and four times she was divorced. Her marriages were truly international. She was married to an American, a Greek, a Russian, and a Frenchman. Her weight problems were almost as favorite a topic among the media as her incredible wealth.

One observer noted that Christina herself realized early on that excessive weight was more an emotional problem than a physical one, and that neither medical care nor money could buy what she needed most: *Someone who truly loved her.*

There is no escaping this truth. Each and every one of us wants to be wanted. We long deeply within the core of our soul for a relationship in which another person will love us the way we long to be loved.

Several years ago Simon and Garfunkel recorded a song which included the words, "I am a rock, I am an island." If that truly represents the feeling of any individual, I think we can reasonably add yet another line to the song: "I am miserable." No one, unless he is deranged, can survive emotionally in isolation from others. No one can live without love. Each of us has embedded within our heart an insatiable desire to be loved unconditionally by another. We want to know and feel the affection someone else has for us.

We long to be loved with no strings attached. We want to be wanted, not "if" or "when" or "on the condition that," but simply for who we are. Few things are as satisfying as knowing that someone else accepts us without first demanding we change—that we measure up to their standards of what a lovable person should be.

Some people, however, are afraid to admit this. They think that to acknowledge such a desire is either sinful or selfish, or perhaps just an indication of weakness in character. They fail to understand that God made us that way. He created us for relationship with others. Philosophers have often described man as a "social animal," one who needs and searches for life in association with other human beings. But the Bible said it long before the philosophers.

Why do you think God said of Adam, "It is not good for the man to be alone" (Genesis 2:18)? Was it because there was too much work in tending the garden for one person to handle? I doubt it. Was it because with only one person there was no hope for propagation of the species? In part. But more important still, I believe it was "bad" for Adam to be alone, because God created him (and us) for *relationship.* Adam's existence was incomplete as long as he lived alone, bereft of the love of a fellow human being.

But you don't have to be married to love and be loved. The Apostle Paul remained single and celibate throughout his life, as many people do. Yet he sustained marvellous, albeit non-sexual, relationships. The kind of love and acceptance I'm describing is found not only in marriage but also in the relationship between parent and child, brother and sister, and among close, intimate friends.

If we are honest with ourselves we're forced to admit that the most severe pain we feel comes from rejection. Ask the child who longs for his parents' approval but hears only biting criticism. Ask the wife whose thirst for marital warmth is met with cool indifference. Nothing hurts quite like the experience of not being wanted as we want. That sort of pain acts like a catalyst, giving fuel to the fear in our souls that if people really knew us as we know ourselves they would find us most unlovable.

I recently saw a vivid example of this on the evening news. The story concerned one of the many tragedies in the aftermath of the Vietnam War. While overseas a disturbing number of American servicemen engaged in immoral and short-lived liaisons with Vietnamese women. The offspring of these sexual encounters are commonly referred to as Amerasians. This particular news broadcast was focusing on the terrible plight in which many of the Amerasian kids find themselves.

No one, literally no one, not even their mothers, wanted them. They were outcasts in their own society. Scorned and mocked as "half-breeds" by their own family and neighbors, they had no place to go. The longing to be loved, simply to be accepted for who they are, was painfully ignored. Rarely has rejection been so horribly and visibly felt. One can see it on their faces. Empty eyes were but a reflection of an unbearable ache in their hearts.

Their only hope for lasting, meaningful relationship, so they thought, was to travel to the United States in search of their natural fathers. Some of them were successful. A few of the fathers were overjoyed at being reunited with the children whom they had perhaps seen only for a few months, some not at all. Other children were not so fortunate. They found themselves as unwanted by their fathers as they were by their mothers and everyone else in southeast Asia. It was a devastating blow.

One teenaged girl received special coverage. Hers was an especially sad case. The news team documented her efforts at contacting her father. When he was finally located he refused even to speak with his daughter. Her hopes of a warm reception, of being embraced in loving arms, were painfully shattered. He declined to answer her phone calls and ignored her letters. The story concluded with the scene of her sitting on the curb, across the street from his home, alone and shut out.

On one level this is a story about the horrors of war and its innocent victims. On another level it is an illustration of what all of us have experienced to one degree or another. This teen-aged girl, not unlike Bridgett, wanted to be wanted. That's all. She longed to be loved by someone who didn't care that she was Amerasian. She longed to be loved by someone who just plain *cared.*

Why did these children feel this way? What can account for their desire? Should we chalk it up to environmental and social influence? Was this little more than learned behavior that with time and counseling can be changed? I don't think so. These young people felt the need for a loving relationship with some-one who cared because that is the way God made them. That is the way God made Bridgett. That is the way God made you and me.

And why shouldn't He have made us that way? After all, that is what God Himself is like! "There is relationship within the very nature of God," writes Crabb. "God is a personal being who exists eternally in a relationship among persons: He is His own community."[2] Therefore, it really shouldn't surprise us that when God created beings in His own image He created them with an indelible desire and capacity for relationship with Himself and other persons. Crabb explains:

> *Each of us fervently wants someone to see us exactly as we are, warts and all, and still accept us.* Because no other human being can ever see all of us, a nagging doubt clouds even the best relationship: What would they think of me if they knew that . . . ? The thought that someone can remain warmly committed to us even with all our faults exposed is utterly inconceivable—yet we long for that experience. We long to be in relationship with someone who

> is strong enough to be constant, someone whose love is untainted by even a trace of manipulative self-interest, someone who really *wants* us. As image-bearers we long for relationship.[3]

Dr. Raymond E. Vath, a recognized expert on eating disorders, has detected what he believes is a vital link between the longing for love and both anorexia nervosa and bulimia. These two problems began to receive widespread public attention following the tragic death of singer Karen Carpenter, whose struggle with anorexia was chronicled in a made-for-television movie.

Anorexia nervosa, explains Vath, is an illness characterized by preoccupation with body weight. This involves an intense fear of gaining weight and extreme forms of behavior directed toward shedding pounds. There is often refusal to eat, except for small portions, and a denial of hunger.

Bulimia, on the other hand, refers to recurrent, compulsive episodes of binge eating followed by self-induced vomiting and/or purging with laxatives and/or diuretics. These are both serious and even life-threatening problems that are most frequently found among white females from middle- and upper-middle-class families.

What does this have to do with our subject, you ask? Well, according to Dr. Vath, one of the major root causes of anorexia and bulimia is *perfectionism.* As the term suggests, a perfectionist has unrealistic and therefore unattainable expectations of herself (or himself). "These individuals," says Vath, "have such extreme rules and definitions by which they measure themselves that nearly everything they attempt becomes a failure, leading to exquisite torment as the feelings of inadequacy and worthlessness grow."[4]

But what causes perfectionism? Why should anyone be prompted to live by such lofty and obviously impossible ideals? Vath suggests that one answer is a false belief he finds in *every* person with an eating disorder: *"I won't be loved unless I'm perfect."*

Where does this belief come from? One common source is the home atmosphere in which a person is raised. The parents of those with eating disorders are usually conscientious, educated, well-meaning people who are high achievers themselves. At least one of them is often intensely health conscious and overly concerned with dieting. The parents, too, tend toward perfectionism and are thus intolerant of error and failure both in themselves and in others.

The principal source, though, is a society in which "value is determined by performance and achievement as measured by salary and bank accounts, by popularity and social position, by other people's opinions of you including how much anger and punishment you receive for your mistakes, and your grade point in school, to name a few."[5]

Anorexia is a baffling and, to most of us, a bizarre affliction. I'm dumbfounded when a twenty-one-year-old, ninety-pound girl bemoans how fat she is! I can't imagine someone feasting on numerous delicacies only to purge herself by self-induced vomiting! What possesses such power that a woman would, quite literally, starve herself to death?

As Dr. Vath is quick to point out, eating disorders are the result of complex behaviors made up of many factors. We must be careful not to reduce the cause to one element. Still, there is no escaping the fact that women who suffer in this way are primarily motivated by a desperate longing for the unconditional affection and acceptance of others. Says Vath, *"I believe that the quest for thinness comes out of the desire to be loved."*[6]

THE PURSUIT OF PURPOSE

But we are not one-dimensional beings. Not only do we long to be loved, we also have a passion for purpose. We desperately want to matter. We long to make an impact on others and the world around us. Just as there is within the human soul a yearning to experience security in a loving relationship with others, there is also a deep and undeniable urge to be a meaningful participant in something of value.

In his earlier books Larry Crabb referred to this two-fold thirst in the human heart as a longing for "security" and "significance." He has since expressed his preference for the terms "relationship" and "impact," lest some find in his model, "a man-centered focus on fulfillment rather than a God-centered emphasis on obedience to Him and preoccupation with His glory."[7] I intend to address this tension between human need and divine glory in the next chapter. Personally, though, I prefer the terms *love* and *purpose*. Having already briefly discussed love, let me say a few words about purpose.

Perhaps an illustration will prove helpful. In his excellent book *Kingdoms in Conflict*, Charles Colson tells of an incident that occurred during World War II in one of Hitler's labor camps. In this particular camp, the Jewish prisoners were forced to work every day in a factory where tons of human waste and other forms of refuse were distilled into alcohol to be used as a fuel additive. It was a nauseating and distasteful task.

One day the factory was destroyed by an Allied bombing raid. Rather than rebuild, the prisoners were ordered to shovel sand into a cart and to haul it from one side of the camp to the other. The next day the same command was issued, and the next day, and the day after, and the day after that. The monotonous, meaningless work began to take its toll. One by one the prisoners began to lose control. Some screamed, some attempted to escape, while others just slowly drifted into insanity. Colson concludes:

> The gruesome lesson is plain: Men will cling to life with dogged resolve while working meaningfully, even if that work supports their hated captors. But purposeless labor soon snaps the mind. You might argue that our need to work was acquired over centuries of evolution. But we must do more than work just to survive; we must do work that has a purpose. Evolution cannot explain this. More plausible is the belief of Jews and Christians that man is a reflection of the nature of a purposeful Creator.[8]

These men could survive mentally only so long as they believed that their lives carried some significance and held some meaning. I am persuaded this is true for every one of us, for the simple reason that we are like God. We are created in the image of a God who Himself thinks and acts purposefully.

Let's again consider the case of Adam. We read in Genesis 1:27-28:

> God created man in his own image, in the image of God he created him; male and female he created them. God blessed them and said to them, "Be fruitful and increase in number; fill the earth and subdue it. Rule over the fish of the sea and the birds of the air and over every living creature that moves on the ground."

I realize it is a speculative question, but what do you think would have happened had God not assigned Adam and Eve a task, in this case the exercise of dominion over the creation? What if God had left Adam and Eve without an expressly stated purpose for their existence? What if God had permitted them merely to wander aimlessly through the garden and through life? Of course, we don't know. But I can't help but believe God intended for Adam (and for us) to experience the thrill of accomplishment, the satisfaction of applying our God-given talents to a meaningful and lasting task.

Because we are created in God's image we not only long for love, we also have an inborn passion for purpose. We not only want to be wanted, we also need to know that our lives, our efforts, are of value to God and to the world over which He has given us dominion.

Be careful, though, that you do not mistakenly confuse what I'm describing with the sinful exaltation of self that infects so much of what we do. This has nothing to do with the egotistical urge to be a "big-shot."

I'm often amused, as well as saddened, when people go to great lengths to have their names publicly displayed or preserved. Those who can afford it bequeath huge sums of money to universities or charitable foundations, hoping to see their name in the cornerstone of a building or in some other way enshrined in the memory of future generations.

None of us is totally immune to this desire. Ray Stedman, a California pastor, describes how he once visited the Natural Bridge of Virginia. There were hundreds of names and initials scratched on the rocks, but one in particular caught his eye. High up on the side, above almost every other name, was scratched, "George Washington"! It appears that even the father of our country felt the urge to gain a kind of immortality by carving his name on a rock.

Have you ever given in to the urge to carve your initials in freshly poured cement? In the summer of 1969, following my senior year in high school, I worked construction for a company in Duncan, Oklahoma. In the parking lot of a nursing home in Meridian, Oklahoma, where we worked, you will find the initials, "C.S.S., 1969." Though my memory of the occasion is imperfect, I must have felt a surge of significance from knowing that my contribution to that building project would not be forgotten.

Of course most of us want more, in our quest for purpose, than just initials in cement. Daniel Taylor, writing in *Christianity Today*, confesses that the only personal fear he can readily identify is "the fear of an insignificant life." The question that haunts him is: "Will it matter, once I am gone, that I was ever here?" He insists that this question is asked in one way or another by every reflective person. It is,

> an outgrowth of the basic human need to feel that we count, that our lives have purpose, that we are not just a temporary configuration of atoms. We may not need statues erected to our memories, but we want to feel we can say at the end of our lives, "My life was worth living. Things are at least slightly better in the world because I was here."[9]

We all feel this gnawing urge for significance, because we are created in the image of a God who Himself is the center and source of all significance. Cats and butterflies and aardvarks don't bother themselves with such questions. Nary an animal on this earth has lost a minute's sleep worrying about whether or not its life is worth living. They just live.

But when you and I "just live," we die. When life is reduced to mere existence we shrivel up inside, wither away, and perish. If our *being* doesn't matter, why *be* at all? Perhaps I'm uninformed, but I've never heard of an animal committing suicide. Despair and depression are unique to the human race precisely because *we are unique.* And when that sense of being uniquely created to be and to do something of lasting value is lost, many people bail out . . . permanently.

"Everyone at this school hates me. . . ."

AN ILLUSTRATION CLOSE TO HOME

Love and purpose. Acceptance and appreciation. Relationship and impact. Whatever words you may choose to describe them, these powerful needs cannot be ignored.

Let me illustrate how these two longings express themselves. One day when Joanna, the younger of our two daughters, was three years old, I heard her and her older sister giggling in the next room. I knew they were up to something. Suddenly, Joanna appeared in front of me, eyes all aglow, holding in her hand a most unlikely work of art. It was a white paper plate with macaroni glued on it. It wasn't a particularly pretty sight. It was just a plain white paper plate. The macaroni wasn't in any special configuration. It wasn't a dog or cat or, thank God, a portrait of my face! Just macaroni glued to a paper plate.

But I will never forget the look on Joanna's face. It isn't that she and Melanie had never before undertaken such creative tasks. This time, however, it happened to be while I was thinking about the subject matter of this chapter. So there she was, looking as if she had consummated work on something that would rival the Mona Lisa. She smiled, held up her masterpiece, and said: "Daddy, look what *I* made! I did it all by myself. And Daddy, guess what? I did it for *you*. It's all yours!"

Now let's be honest. In the great and grand scheme of things a paper plate with macaroni glued to it may not seem to amount to much. In a world full of war and hunger and moral issues calling for resolution, what Joanna held in her hand was of little if any significance. But as far as *she* was concerned, *nothing* in this world mattered more. Why?

How do you explain the thrill she felt in having made something she thought was a valuable contribution to my life? While not denying the influence of an older sister and other social factors, I believe she responded this way because that's how God made her. I was seeing concrete evidence in her life of an image-bearer, created for loving relationship and meaningful purpose. When I reached down and picked her up, telling her how much I appreciated her efforts and the beautiful work she had done, the cake was iced. No one needed to tell me what she felt. I could see it in her eyes.

This thirst for love and purpose is basic to human nature. It is part of what it is to be created in the image of God. The desire for security and significance, or for relationship and impact is a fundamental constituent of what it is to be human.

This doesn't mean all our desires are of equal importance. There are longings in the human heart that are undeniably less crucial than those for love and purpose. For example, most of us want our lives to be free from debilitating obstacles and problems. We like the convenience, comfort, and ease that money can often buy. On Saturdays we prefer good weather to bad. We would rather eat steak and lobster than a BLT. We desire good health for ourselves and for our children. When these needs go unmet, we experience noticeable irritation and discomfort. But we'll survive.

There is an "intermediate" level of desires, somewhere between the hope that our car doesn't break down and the thirst for significance as a human being. For example, you desire lasting and meaningful friendship with the people around you. It is your hope and prayer that your aged father and mother do not experience prolonged suffering in their later years. If such desires are not met, you'll feel something more intense than mere discomfort. Painful distress and disappointment set in. Such grief and emotional agony are frequently the cause of severe depression and other problems. But for all the anguish of soul, there is hope for recovery. All is not lost.

It's a different story, however, when the longing of our heart for love and purpose goes unmet. When the deep-seated, divinely created urge for relationship and impact is deprived of fulfillment, discomfort and distress are hardly adequate terms to describe how we feel. *Disaster* is the only word that conveys the result. Our lives fall apart. Our hearts sink within us. Our souls wither away.

We lose all sense of self-respect and dignity. Whatever self-esteem we once had is now horribly disfigured.

Here is what I want you to understand: God never promised to make the sun shine on Saturdays. He never promised that you would forever be healthy and wealthy. Contrary to the claims of many today, the Bible does not say that God will always insulate us from the discomfort and distress of living in a fallen, sinful world. Of course, on occasion He may. When God does bless us with physical health and financial resources and moments of ease, comfort, and peace, our only proper response is one of unending gratitude. But not even a grateful heart can guarantee that such blessings will always come our way.

On this, however, you may go to the bank: God and God alone can and will at all times and in every circumstance fulfill your deep longing for love and purpose. My most fervent desire to be loved as I want to be loved will be satisfied by God alone. My wife can't do it. No husband could ask for a more loving, giving wife than mine. But she will be the first to tell you what you already know from Scripture. She is a sinner. Therefore she will occasionally fail me, even as I fail her.

My parents could not love me the way I was made to be loved. Again, a son couldn't ask for better and more godly parents than my own. I thank God for them. But they too are sinners. My children and friends and other family members cannot want me the way I want to be wanted.

Why not? Because no matter how much they all may try, they are all fallen creatures. To some degree each of them places conditions and qualifications on their love for me. You see, my acceptance with everyone other than God is dependent on my performance. My acceptance with God is based on *Christ's* performance, and He was perfect! The day may come (God forbid) when my wife leaves me, my children rebel against me, and my parents disown me. But the great Triune God of Scripture will never leave me nor forsake me (Romans 8:31-39, Hebrews 13:5).

Likewise, my most basic need to be useful, to be appreciated for doing something of lasting significance in this world will be met only in Christ. You may have recently lost your job. Your new Cadillac is gone, replaced by a run-down Chevy. It seems as if no one has need of your skills. You are unemployed and feel useless. You've hit rock bottom.

But take heart: The Rock at the bottom is Christ! *You are always useful to Him.* Though stripped of all earthly treasures, you are a vital and essential contributor to the purpose and plan of God. There are no insignificant people in the Body of Christ (1 Corinthians 12:14-31, Ephesians 4:16). Though your world may be crumbling, the thirst in your soul for security and significance is forever fulfilled in Christ. In the rest of this book, we'll look deeper at this dependency on Christ and how it works in our lives.

Let me summarize the message of this chapter. Everything, and I mean *everything*, necessary to satisfy our deepest longings is found in Christ. He alone loves us as we long to be loved. He alone needs us as we need to be needed. We are secure in His love, significant in His plan. The most unlovely are loveable in His sight. The most useless are of profound importance to His eternal purpose.

We still live in a fallen world. We will still be let down and disappointed by fallen people. But no amount of discomfort or distress need ever destroy us as persons. For in Christ we have all we need.

It saddens me to say this, but Joanna is eventually going to learn (if she hasn't already) that her daddy is not altogether reliable. She is going to discover that, try as he might, he is incapable of fully accepting and appreciating her in the way she desires. Some day when he is tired and irritable, macaroni glued to a paper plate will only be a nuisance. Instead of a warm and affectionate hug, she will hear him say, "Not now, I'm too tired for that sort of nonsense!" or "Please move out of the way, I'm watching the ball game." She'll learn one of the most painful lessons of life, that her daddy can't always meet her need for love and purpose. But hopefully her daddy will be able to teach her that Christ *can* meet that need!

So what makes us tick? To put it simply, we are motivated in most of what we do and in the relationships we sustain with others by *a God-given hunger to experience love and purpose in our lives*. And we will do anything within our power, both good and evil, to see that we achieve that love and that purpose. We will take whatever steps we must to protect ourselves from the painful disappointment of feeling *in*secure (unloved) and *in*significant (unnecessary). Virtually every problem we encounter, as well as the many burdens we bear, are due in some way to an attempt to satisfy that longing through some thing, some activity, or some person other than Jesus Christ.

But before we take up the question of how problems develop, I need to address two questions that often arise. Many of you are asking even now: "In all this talk of human need and human fulfillment, where is God and His glory?" That's a good question. I'll try to respond with a good answer in the next chapter.

Just as profound a question that many others are asking now is, "How can this work for me? How can I really *feel* and *experience* this great love and purpose?" Be patient, my friend, this too will be answered in the pages ahead.

FOUR

But It Sounds So Selfish!

Do you remember the mythological character named Narcissus? He was the son of the river god Cephisus in ancient Greek mythology. As the story goes, Narcissus was an extremely handsome young man, the Tom Cruise of the mythological world. The problem was that he knew it, and his lack of humility was destined to get him into trouble.

On several occasions Narcissus arrogantly scorned advances from the young girls who loved him. One of them, Echo, was so deeply offended by his cold disdain that all but her voice faded away. The gods were angered by this and punished Narcissus by causing him to fall in love with his own reflection in a pool of water.

The self-obsessed lunacy of Narcissus, unfortunately, did not die when he did. As one modern writer has observed:

> There once was a nymph named Narcissus,
> Who thought himself very delicious;
> So he stared like a fool
> At his face in a pool,
> And his folly today is still with us.[1]

EGO OR ELOHIM?

Some people who began reading this book never made it to this chapter. They said to themselves, if not after chapters 1 and 2, then certainly after chapter 3, *Just as I thought; another book on 'self'! Self-esteem, self-love, self-fulfillment. My needs, my desires, my longings. It's narcissism, pure and simple!*

I know that's what many are saying because that is precisely how I would have reacted only a year or two ago. I am still deeply disturbed by the human-centered focus found in many of our evangelical churches. The last thing in the world I intend by this book is to shift your eyes from Christ to self. If anything, my goal is the opposite.

Why, then, has so much been said about *human* needs? Why all the emphasis on the satisfaction of human desires and longings? Shouldn't we as Christians stop focusing on ourselves and get down to the business of obeying and glorifying God? These are perfectly legitimate questions. Let's carefully consider some possible answers.

A few people, even in the professing Christian community, insist that the primary motivation in all that we do is *self*. All that I do, they claim, is done to satisfy or to fulfill my personal needs. The glory of God is at best a secondary consideration. God-centered or theocentric thinking, so they argue, may actually be detrimental to the development of healthy self-esteem.

Others, at the opposite end of the theological spectrum, insist that I should ignore and deny my personal needs. *Any* regard for self is sinful and selfish. If a thought or deed is to be virtuous, it must be devoid of any concern for the immediate or long-term impact on the individual. To the degree that I am motivated by self, God is diminished.

But are these our only two options? *Either* we ignore God and satisfy self, *or* we ignore self and glorify God? I hope not.

Why must we conclude that the fulfillment of our longings, on the one hand, and the exaltation of God, on the other, are mutually exclusive? Instead of approaching this question as if it demanded an "either/or" response, perhaps a "both/and" approach would prove more fruitful: "I will glorify *God* by satisfying *my* personal needs *in Him*." In this approach, God is honored and exalted as the One in whom alone the desires of the human heart may be met.

Does this both/and approach still sound selfish? It is obviously based on the assumption that certain human desires are legitimate, and that an attempt to satisfy them does not necessarily detract from the glory of God. Take for instance our basic human longing for love and purpose. Is there anything inherently sinful in that desire? Is it spiritually and morally wrong to want to be wanted? Is it contrary to God's will to yearn for purpose and impact? Many Christians are convinced that it is. They pray that God would purge their hearts of any and all concern for self. To think at all of one's desires precludes the possibility of thinking about God.

When Joanna came to me with her macaroni glued to a paper plate, zealous for appreciation and approval, should I have gently rebuked her and insisted that she repent? Was I a witness to an expression of her fallen flesh? Or was what she did and desired simply a product of what it means to be created in the image of God? Did I fail as a father in not taking the opportunity to teach her something about the nature of sin and egoism? Or was she merely feeling and acting in accordance with the way God made her?

I am persuaded that her longing for love and purpose was an altogether legitimate expression of what it is to be human. Desire, per se, is not necessarily sinful. God created us with desires. He fashioned us in His image as people who yearn in the depths of our souls for loving relationship and lasting impact.

It is Buddhism, not biblical Christianity, that condemns desire. One of the four noble truths in Buddhist philosophy is that the cause of suffering is desire. When your desire is not satisfied, you suffer. The way to put an end to suffering, therefore, is to snuff out desire. Instead of increasing satisfaction, work at decreasing desire. Reduce your longings to a minimum and the pain of dissatisfaction will disappear.

Although some may find that to be a helpful solution, it is utterly foreign to biblical Christianity. Of course there are some desires that are sinful. The desire for illicit sex, the desire to inflict pain on the innocent, greed, jealousy, and envy, just to mention a few, are clearly prohibited in Scripture. But the Bible nowhere provides a blanket condemnation of desire. The crucial question is not, "should we desire?" but, "what and why do we desire, and how do we go about fulfilling our desire?"

ENJOYING GOD

The desire to experience love and purpose is *the God-given product of Creation*, not of the Fall. God made us needful of love and purpose precisely in order that He might be glorified when we experience the satisfaction of our longings in Him.

In his book *Desiring God*, John Piper suggests a slight revision in the Westminster Confession that illustrates what I mean. Instead of affirming that, "the chief end of man is to glorify God *and* to enjoy Him forever," Piper prefers to say that, "the chief end of man is to glorify God *by* enjoying Him forever."[2] Our chief end in life is still the same: To glorify God in all we do and say. But now the principal way we do this is by finding in Him and in Him alone the joy and satisfaction for which our souls so desperately yearn. If Piper is correct, and I believe he is, we need no longer fear that the virtue of our actions is lessened to the degree that we are motivated by a desire for our own pleasure.

How else can we explain the appeal Jesus made to our desires as grounds for faith? He frequently appealed to our spiritual and emotional thirst when preaching (see John 6:32-35, 7:37-39). If you are hungry, come to Christ and He will feed you. If you are thirsty, come to Christ and He will soothe your parched and dry soul. "Far from condemning our hunger and thirst as self-oriented," says Larry Crabb, "our Lord appeals to them as good reason for coming to Him."[3] Are you weary and worn out and crushed beneath the oppressive weight of your sins and the burdens life imposes? If so, come to Christ. "Take my yoke upon you," He says, "and learn from me, for I am gentle and humble in heart, and you will find rest for your souls" (Matthew 11:29).

A truly remarkable statement by our Lord in the Sermon on the Mount is an excellent example of what I have in mind. He first pronounces a blessing upon all who are willing to suffer persecution and slander for the sake of righteousness. He actually tells them to "rejoice and be glad" (Matthew 5:12). Some find that strange (others would say it is downright masochistic). But look at the reason why Jesus says what He does: "Rejoice and be glad, because great is *your reward* in heaven" (emphasis added). It is in anticipation of a personal heavenly reward that we are to find strength to stand up under persecution.

I don't see how we can deny the fact that Jesus appeals to our self-interest as a reason for believing in Him. Concern for oneself, for one's spiritual and emotional and physical welfare, is sinful only if our efforts to find satisfaction look to some thing or some person other than Christ.

"The Scriptures," Crabb says, "acknowledge that we all long deeply for satisfaction without ever hinting at a rebuke for our feeling those desires. We must say it clearly: It is not wrong to desire deep joy in our souls. A longing for happiness does not make us selfish. To deny self does not require that we stop caring whether we're happy or not, or that we somehow must nobly rise above an interest in our own well-being."[4] As Piper has said, "seeking one's own happiness is not a sin; it is a simple given in human nature. It is a law of the human heart as gravity is a law of nature."[5]

For some time now I have been counselling a young lady who struggles with an intense and often debilitating conviction of guilt. What is the sin for which she feels guilty? Her answer: "I want to be happy." She feels selfish and sub-Christian for merely giving thought to her own desire for joy. Tragically, she's not alone in this. No wonder we have so many miserable, sour-faced Christians in the Church.

What I have told her is that sin does not consist in the desire for love and purpose and the joy they yield, but in the willful determination to find them apart from a saving, dependent relationship with Jesus Christ. Let me say it again: We sin when we seek satisfaction for self *in* self. It is *good* to find satisfaction for self in Christ!

Even Adam, before the Fall, was a dependent being. He was created with a God-given thirst and hunger for loving relationship and lasting meaning in life. Human need is not a consequence of the Fall. It is a constituent part of being human. God created us that way for His own glory. He is exalted and magnified when our deep personal longings to experience love and purpose are fulfilled in and by Him. Because we are created in the divine image, we thirst. Because we are sinners, determined to make life work without Him, we look to quench it in all the wrong places.

God wants you to want! That's because He knows that He

alone is capable of supplying what you lack. He longs to be the pool of refreshing water at which you quench your thirst, the table at which you feast to fill your hungry soul. Do not be ashamed or fearful of your desire to be loved unconditionally and eternally. Your Creator made you that way so that He would be glorified when His love for you is revealed and recognized as the only love that lasts.

Do not let anyone condemn you for your desire to matter. As R. C. Sproul has said, "Deeply ensconced in the marrow of our bones is the aspiration for significance. The phrase is abstract but it defines the clamoring beat of every human heart for self-esteem. We want our lives to count. We yearn to believe that in some way we are important."[6] That's no guarantee that people in this world will acknowledge your value as a person, but it is a reminder that God has ordained a plan in which you are to play a vital, valuable, and indispensable role.

God is delighted when we are delighted in Him. So don't deny your desire for delight. Instead, glut yourself in God! Do you long for joy? Good!

> You have made known to me the path of life;
> you will fill me with joy in your presence,
> with eternal pleasures at your right hand. (Psalm 16:11)

The world says, "Delight yourself!" The Bible says, "Delight yourself *in the LORD* and he will give you *the desires of your heart*" (Psalm 37:4, emphasis added). There is an eternity of difference between the two.

WHAT ABOUT SELF-DENIAL?

I know what you're thinking, and you're right: On the surface it does seem as if what Jesus said in Mark 8:34-37 puts an end to all concern for self:

> If anyone would come after me, he must deny himself and take up his cross and follow me. For whoever wants to save his life will lose it, but whoever loses his life for me and for

the gospel will save it. What good is it for a man to gain the whole world, yet forfeit his soul? Or what can a man give in exchange for his soul?

When Jesus calls upon you to "deny" yourself, He does not mean that you should neglect or be indifferent toward your emotional, physical, or personal needs. He doesn't mean, "When you feel hungry, ignore and repress the urge to eat." Far less is He suggesting that we abandon all concern for our spiritual and emotional welfare. Jesus is in fact appealing to our sense of personal need and the concern we ought to have for the condition of our souls. Let me try to explain what seems contradictory.

If we are not concerned for our "selves," if we care little or not at all for what happens to us, these words of Jesus would be senseless. Why do you think Jesus calls on us to deny ourselves and follow Him? It's because if we do not, we shall die. Why does He tell us to "lose" our lives (literally, our "souls") for His sake? It is because that's the only way we can "save" them.

In other words, Jesus knows that each of us wants what is best for our own "selves," for our "souls," and therefore makes His urgent appeal on that basis. He says it somewhat paradoxically: "If you really want to do what is best for your 'self,' deny your 'self'!" That is to say, the best thing you can obtain is eternal life. But the consequence may well be the loss of earthly life and the pleasures of sin it offers.

What good is it to you or what personal benefit or profit can come, from enhancing your physical life if it costs you your eternal, spiritual life? To quote John Piper again, "Self-denial is never a virtue in itself. It has value precisely in proportion to the superiority of the reality embraced above the one desired. Self-denial that is not based on a desire for some superior goal will become the ground of boasting."[7]

It is your personal desire for the greater blessing of eternal and spiritual life to which Jesus appeals in asking that you sacrifice the lesser blessing of temporal and physical life. His point is that it is better for you that you deny yourself than that you don't. Jesus is not denouncing all concern for self, but the sinful concern for self *that shuts Him out.*

There is no greater profit for self than that which comes with following Christ. To refuse to follow Christ is to deny oneself the greatest blessing possible! So Jesus is saying: "Deny and renounce all your sinful attempts to satisfy your needs through self, fame, fortune, earthly praise, or whatever else on which you have been relying. Instead, do yourself a favor! Follow Me, for I can give you what nothing and no one else can."

If we ever hope to obtain for ourselves what is ultimately the best (and it is okay to hope that we will), we must deny any hope or expectation of finding it in what we are or can do or in what this world might provide. We must crucify the spirit of pride which says, "I can make it without Christ." We must renounce any attempt to gain *in and through* self what is most needful *for* self.

But I do not hear Jesus telling us to ignore our needs or to repress the longings of our soul. Quite to the contrary, He appears to tell us precisely how to fulfill them! His paradoxical appeal to deny ourselves is based on the fact that we are intensely (and justifiably) concerned about what will happen to us if we don't.

C. S. Lewis explained it this way:

> The New Testament has lots to say about self-denial, but not about self-denial as an end in itself. We are told to deny ourselves and to take up our crosses in order that we may follow Christ; and nearly every description of what we shall ultimately find if we do so contains an appeal to desire.
>
> If there lurks in most modern minds the notion that to desire our own good and earnestly to hope for the enjoyment of it is a bad thing, I submit that this notion has crept in from Kant and the Stoics and is no part of the Christian faith. Indeed, if we consider the unblushing promises of reward and the staggering nature of the rewards promised in the Gospels [see, for example, Mark 10:28-31], it would seem that Our Lord finds our desires not too strong, but too weak. We are half-hearted creatures, fooling about with drink and sex and ambition when infinite joy is offered us, like an ignorant child who wants to go on making mud pies in a slum because he cannot imagine what is meant by the offer of a holiday at the sea. We are far too easily pleased.[8]

Please don't be misled. I am not portraying God as merely a tool or instrument to be used for the pleasure He provides. The pleasure God provides for thirsty souls is God Himself. *He* is our exceeding great reward! We seek no higher satisfaction than that which *is* God.

Few things in life provide me with greater joy than when my daughters find in my arms the love and protection they long to experience. I do not feel slighted when they express their desire for warmth and affection. I'm honored by it! I do not accuse them of being disdainful of me and concerned only for themselves. Would you have me rebuke them for enjoying what only I as their father can provide? Is it not in the satisfaction of their need that my adequacy as a parent is made manifest? Imagine, then, the depth of joy in the heart of our heavenly Father when we, His children, find in Him our all in all.

A PAINFUL WAY TO MAKE A POINT

Let me bring this to a close by asking how you would have responded to a situation I recently faced. It isn't pleasant, but it does make the point.

When Mary Ann first told me her story I was amazed at how matter-of-factly she spoke. I realized later it was the only way she could survive her memories. To permit herself to feel the impact of what she described was more than she could handle at that time.

The list of those who had sexually abused Mary Ann is long and frightening: brothers, an uncle, a next-door-neighbor, a friend's father, and others. On the one occasion she found courage to tell what happened, her mother ignored the tears and blamed it on her "seductive" appearance. Mary Ann never mentioned it again. Silence was preferable to the pain of rejection and blame.

Perhaps the most devastating incident didn't involve physical contact . . . but the abuse was not for that reason any less painful. When Mary Ann was in the eighth grade her father returned home drunk, as was his custom. The words she heard echoing from her parents' bedroom are difficult for her to describe, and difficult for me to repeat. After resisting his advances, Mary Ann's mother screamed: "If you want it, go get it from that bitch daughter of yours!" Had he chosen to enter her room (which he didn't), Mary Ann was as prepared as any thirteen-year-old girl could be. She waited with a knife tightly gripped in her hand.

One wonders how a little girl survives this kind of childhood.[9] Mary Ann almost didn't. She became pregnant in high school and gave up her child for adoption. Wrists were slashed and pills were swallowed. She was in and out of mental hospitals, in and out of abusive relationships, in and out of a marriage that knew nothing of love.

There's more, but I see no need to prolong the discomfort we feel in hearing such tragic details. But I do have good reason for telling you about Mary Ann. As this book goes to press she is beginning the arduous but ultimately rewarding task of dealing with the damage to her soul. The wounds are deep, but the Lord Jesus Christ is a gentle physician.

Mary Ann wants her story told. So do I. Here is why. Her soul, as well as her body, has been raped. Every human emotion has been trampled. She was never permitted to cry as a child, never allowed to relax in the arms of a loving father or to know the thrill of his smiling approval. Putting trust in people brought betrayal, enjoying life produced shame. She never experienced the satisfaction of personal achievement or the warmth of family affection.

She never felt enjoyed, only exploited; never needed, only used; never cherished, only rejected for failing to live up to impossible expectations. Her opinions never mattered, her choices were ignored, her desires went unfulfilled.

What would you have me say to her? Something like, "That's just terrible, Mary Ann. What you need to do is . . . pray about it . . . just obey God . . . forgive and forget. After all, it's in the past." Would you have me tell her that anything beyond this panders to human need to the detriment of divine glory? You may not like this, but my opinion is that such "counsel" is hardly less abusive than much of what she experienced as a child.

Don't think I'm suggesting that prayer and obedience and forgiveness are unimportant. They are absolutely essential to Mary Ann's recovery. But responding to her cry with such insensitive simplicity does neither her nor God any good.

The longings of her soul, now so horribly disfigured, were created by God for His glory. Suppressing her pain deprives the Lord of the opportunity to display the wealth of His healing grace. If Mary Ann is to feel the loving embrace of her heavenly Father she must face the horror of earlier rejection. There is in her heart an emotional vacuum that God longs to fill. But how, if our "counsel" treats such human need with disdain and rebuke?

Mary Ann's need is no obstacle to God's glory. It is, in fact, the occasion for it. That is, assuming you and I do not callously accuse her of selfish preoccupation with her own pain.

GOD-CENTERED LIVING

We live in an age where man is made the measure of all things. Man's will has become a law unto itself. Man's glory has become the goal of every endeavor. I deplore the attempt by some to recast our religious mind into an anthropocentric (human centered) mold. God is and must forever remain both the source and center of our spiritual focus. We must resist any attempt to place man at the hub of the universe if it means relegating God to some remote spot on the periphery.

But in our zeal to be theocentric (God-centered) in both thought and deed, we must not ignore or suppress the hunger of the human heart. For in doing so we rob God of opportunity to manifest His incomparable beneficence. It is precisely in filling the empty heart and slaking the thirsty soul that God's bountiful supply is released.

Knee-jerk reactions to any mention of human need can easily boomerang into depriving God of the recognition that is rightfully His. Human longing is neither to be ignored nor made an end in itself. Like everything else in life, it is a means to a more ultimate goal: The glory of God.

I wrote this chapter to answer the question: "In all this talk of me and my desires and my needs, where is God and His glory?" I hope the answer is now evident. God is both the Creator and Consummation of my need. *From Him* comes my thirst for love and purpose. *In Him* my thirst is assuaged. And *to Him* is all the glory as the only One in whom my life finds its fulfillment.

FIVE

Do We Blame It All on Sin?

I am a mechanical idiot. Machines and gadgets and household appliances are a complete mystery to me. I'm the fulfillment of every repair man's wildest dreams. My philosophy is, "If it breaks, hire someone to fix it. If he's unavailable, do without!"

When I was growing up in a small town in central Oklahoma, my friends couldn't wait for my birthday to come around not so much because they enjoyed a party, but because of the model airplanes people would send me as gifts. Invariably I would pass the planes on to the neighborhood gang. As far as I'm concerned, the most frightening words in the English language are *some assembly required.* I can't explain it. All I know is that the mere thought of nuts and bolts, pulleys and pistons, makes me sweat. I get literally nauseated at the prospect of having to look under the hood of my car.

But don't think I'm frustrated by my mechanical ineptitude. I like it. I don't *want* to know how machines work. Ignorance is bliss!

My lack of curiosity, however, doesn't apply in all areas of life. There are some things in which I have a burning interest. *People,* for example. I am fascinated by human behavior. Why do men and women act the way they do? What motivates them? Where do they get their ideas, and why are they often willing to die for them? What are the causes of their joy and their despair, their love and their hatred? Why do they have problems, and how can those problems be solved? These are some of the questions that excite me.

Nuclear reactors and space-flight simulators and artificial hearts are complex devices, but nothing can compare with the complexity and mystery of the human soul. Machines, no matter the size or shape, are nothing more than creations of creatures. People, on the other hand, are creations of the Creator. We are fashioned in the image of an infinite and ultimately incomprehensible God, something that cannot be said of radios and lawn mowers and microchips.

In chapter 3, I suggested that a crucial prerequisite for helping people who hurt is an understanding of "what makes them tick." If you and I hope to bear one another's burdens, it would help to understand why those burdens exist. Blaming it on sin is legitimate, but it is also simplistic. We need to know what it is about sin in the human soul that leads to problems in daily living and in relationships. And we need to know what it is about the human soul that permits sin to wreak such incredible emotional havoc.

When the air conditioner in my home breaks down during a heat wave, it is comforting to know that the repairman knows something about compressors and freon. When your child develops a severe abdominal pain, it helps for the pediatrician to know on which side the appendix is found! And when your best friend is fighting a daily war with depression and bitterness, and pours out her heart to you, the effectiveness of your counsel to her is largely dependent on your ability to discern the source of the spiritual breakdown.

The treatment of any problem, whether mechanical, biological, or emotional, is only as good as the accuracy of the diagnosis. That is why this chapter is important. In it I want to sketch out some ideas concerning the source of the problems we encounter in life. Perhaps then we will be better prepared to help others (and ourselves) to bear life's burdens.

YOU ARE WHAT YOU BELIEVE

The critical point made in chapter 3 is that people are primarily motivated by the urge to satisfy their deep longings for security and significance. We may not always think in those terms, but the fact remains that we long to experience the emotional, interpersonal warmth that comes from secure relationships in which we are wanted and loved unconditionally.

Equally powerful in shaping our lives is the yearning for significance. We want to matter. God created you and me with a natural desire to make a difference in our world. We want to know that we are sufficiently competent to make a lasting contribution to something of value. *We want to be worth something to someone.*

Perhaps no time is more critical in our development as individuals (aside from conversion) than when we begin to learn what it takes to win the love and appreciation of people we value. During our childhood years, or more suddenly at some later stage, each of us adopts a set of assumptions or beliefs that explain how we can most effectively satisfy our desire for love and our longing for purpose.

Kevin Huggins has written a helpful book describing how this understanding develops in adolescents.[1] He points out that, once an adolescent becomes aware of the need for love and a sense of purpose, she begins subconsciously to ask herself two basic questions: "What kind of person do I have to be to get someone to want me and love me?" and, "What kind of person do I have to be to accomplish something significant that others will value?"

Huggins says these questions "reveal what the human personality really longs to find in a relationship. The first guides the adolescent in constructing a plan that is calculated to win her love; the second moves her toward a plan that is calculated to win her impact."[2]

The influence of one's parents on how a child answers these questions is of immense, if not paramount, importance.[3] It is frightening for me to think that the way I live is having such a profound impact on my two daughters. There simply is no escaping the fact that my efforts to satisfy my own thirst for security and significance will be reproduced in their lives. Crabb says it clearly:

> If we really believe that money or achievement brings significance or that compliments and attractive clothing bring

> security, we can prate all we want about the joys of knowing Jesus. Our kids will learn to depend on what we really are depending on for our satisfaction in life. No amount of teaching, family devotions, or trips to church will effectively counter the message we convey by our lives. Children will learn that their needs can be met if they reach the same goal for which their parents strive.[4]

Parents are not the only source for instilling these beliefs in the minds of young people. Peers and the media are also powerful forces for molding the mind. We are bombarded daily by the voice of television, insisting that human value is dependent on driving an especially fast and flashy sports car, or using a cologne or shampoo bearing the name of some particular celebrity. If you want to be worth anything, if you ever hope to experience "true love," use this brand of toothpaste, bathe with that kind of soap, wear these clothes, and be certain that your body resembles his or hers!

The tragic fact is that ours is a world in which brains, beauty, and brawn are the measure of human worth.[5] The message is loud and clear: "No one is going to love the stupid or the clumsy or the poor or the unattractive. If you want the people in your world to sit up and take notice, here's what you must do, . . . here's the kind of person you must become. . . ."

The way you and I conduct ourselves and relate to our own peers communicates a world of impressions to our children. Are they learning the lesson that love is dependent on all A's and being selected for the lead in the school play? Does your son believe that his value to you is enhanced by his making the first team? When you work fourteen hours a day, are you subtly telling him that financial success is essential for personal worth? What is your "plain Jane" daughter to think when she observes how greatly impressed you are with the beauty of that girl who lives down the block?

The point is this: Each of us, in response to a variety of influences, constructs a belief system that defines what will satisfy our longing for security and significance. We conduct our lives in constant pursuit of whatever embodies our sense of personal worth. It is what Crabb calls the sin of "misplaced dependency." We nurture within ourselves a reliance on everything other than the One who alone can quench the thirst of our souls.

And we invariably reap a frightful harvest. For virtually every non-physiological problem we encounter may be traced to an attempt to satisfy our basic longings through some means other than Jesus Christ.

It may sound simplistic. But I still believe it is true. We live on the basis of the belief, whenever and however acquired, that we can find happiness and wholeness apart from Christ. We try to get this happiness from our mate, our children, our career, our money, the approval and acceptance of our peers, sex, intellectual and athletic achievement, or whatever else we believe can fill the hunger in our hearts. Sin has deceived us into thinking that other people or other things can give us what only Christ can.

WHAT IS YOUR GOAL?

It stands to reason that once a person is persuaded concerning what it takes to get his needs met, he will begin doing the things which he believes will most quickly and effectively meet those needs. If I believe (wrongly) that significance is dependent upon the size of my bank account, my goal in life will be to make as much money as I can. My problem, however, is not so much financial greed as it is spiritual thirst. Money is little more than a material instrument by which I hope to affirm my importance as a person.

A wife may have as one of her principal goals never to be criticized for her housework, believing (wrongly) that the love she so desperately needs from her husband is dependent on always having his approval. Thus what appears to be submissiveness is, in reality, her calculated scheme to manipulate her husband into giving her the compliments on which she believes her worth as a woman depends.

Or perhaps a mother has dedicated herself to the physical and intellectual perfection of her children, not so much out of concern for them, but based on her belief that model children will bring the social acceptance she secretly cherishes. To lose face with her friends, she believes (wrongly), would be to lose her significance as a person.

Our behavior is invariably a reflection of the goals we have set for ourselves. Little if any of what we do lacks a motive. Goals always govern actions. These goals, in turn, are a product of our beliefs as to what is necessary to satisfy our most fundamental need for security in our relationships and significance in our work.

Often our goals are forged in the fires of a particularly painful relationship. We may feel betrayed by someone in whom we had placed our trust. It may be the agony of abandonment or some personal loss that leaves us feeling alone and unappreciated. Once we've endured the discomfort of such a moment we are determined to do whatever is necessary to make sure it doesn't happen again. We are driven by one all-consuming goal: To minimize the pain. Our instinct for self-preservation is suddenly put in gear as we concoct a scheme that we think will keep us safe. "I'll do anything, I'll say anything, I'll become anything if it will keep you from failing me as you did before. I'm determined never again to be put in such a vulnerable position in our relationship."

THE FRUSTRATION OF FAILURE

But what happens when such goals are not attained? There frequently ensues a disturbing array of debilitating emotional effects. We are wracked with guilt and self-denigration when our efforts to achieve our high goals fall short. If someone else get's in our way and is responsible for our failure, we are provoked to anger and bitterness and resentment.

Sometimes the goal is reasonable enough, but the prospect of trying and failing is so intense that we are paralyzed with fear. So we do nothing. The result in this case is often anxiety, hopelessness, perhaps even despair. Regardless of the cause, when goals are not reached we suffer the emotional consequences.

At other times, the failure to achieve our misguided goals simply provokes our anger. An embarrassing incident that occurred not too long ago will illustrate my point. My wife of nineteen years, Ann, has always been a source of encouragement for me when it comes to my preaching. No matter how low I might feel after preaching poorly, I can always count on her to stroke my wounded ego. On this particular Sunday I had delivered what I thought was one of my best sermons. It had to rank in the top ten, among the all-time best. It was the kind of sermon that makes an egotistical and immature preacher wonder how the church ever got along without him. I was puffed up bigger than a bullfrog.

As Ann stood in the kitchen preparing Sunday lunch, I walked in expecting her to inflate the balloon of my ever-expanding pride just a little bit more. "Well, honey, what did you think about my sermon?" It seemed like such an innocent question, so casually spoken. Her response would have punctured a hole in the Goodyear blimp! "I didn't hear a word you said," came her startling reply. "I was too distracted by the way you kept touching your nose." (She didn't really say "touching." It's a euphemism I've chosen to preserve my own dignity!)

I was stunned. I simply couldn't believe it. Here I had preached a powerfully moving message and all Ann came away with was a tally on how many times I had "touched" my nose! To say that I was deflated that Sunday afternoon is putting it mildly. Besides my obvious embarrassment, I was angry! No, I was enraged! For days following the conversation in the kitchen I fumed. Her apology for being so blunt (even though she didn't owe me one) was dutifully accepted. But my anger and bitterness continued to intensify.

After a while I began to feel badly about the way I had responded to Ann's comment. She had not intended to hurt me, but had spoken out of concern for my effectiveness as a minister. As time passed I began to understand the reason for my angry reaction. It gradually dawned on me that my goal in regularly asking her opinion of my sermons was not entirely selfless and spiritual.

My concern each Sunday should have been: "Was God glorified in His Word today? Were His people encouraged and edified by my exposition of Scripture?" But my actual motive had been to elicit from Ann positive, reassuring approval of my efforts; I had been depending on her praise to affirm my significance as a minister of God's Word. The routine Sunday inquiry was little more than a manipulative strategy for winning the acclaim I found essential for my personal worth as a man. When Ann blocked that goal, my angry and bitter response was inevitable.

I realize this is a pitifully brief and perhaps overly simplistic explanation of why many good Christian men and women are struggling today. But I'm persuaded that its broad outlines are both biblically and experientially true. I am certainly not suggesting that all problems are this easily understood and overcome. We must not forget that fallen creatures, which we are, cannot escape the inevitable disappointments that come from living in a fallen world, as we do. Paul made it clear that we will continue to "groan" in our humanness until Christ returns (Romans 8:18-25). But this does not mean that believers must lead lives crippled by depression, guilt, anger, bitterness, and despair. Such an emotional burden is usually the consequence of our failure to attain wrongly chosen goals, goals that reflect our mistaken notions about how to fill the emptiness in our hearts.

When our brothers and sisters in Christ are living each day under the oppressive weight of such struggles, *the Bible says we must come to their aid*. We are to bear those burdens with and for them. We are to counsel, encourage and minister to them in such a way that their load is lightened. We are to do more than sympathize with their pain. We are *to share it* so that it may be lessened. We are to help them solve the root problems that cause such pain.

Now that we have a general idea of why that pain exists, we can proceed to answer the question: How may I help temper my brothers' and sisters' pain with the joy of Christ? How can I practice mercy?

SIX

The Beginnings of Mercy

Let's look back at where we've been. I have tried to direct our attention to four crucial truths.

First, people are hurting and struggling worse than we think, appearances notwithstanding. Beneath the veneer of visible "holiness" their hearts are often burdened by problems and fears and destructive feelings of which they alone are aware.

Tragically, people would often rather continue to feel the pain of their problems than face what they believe is the humiliation of exposure. "Better to suffer in secret than for others to discover that *I'm not* what *they are*! Better to live quietly with my anguish than be perceived as having failed God!"

The Church is largely to blame for nurturing this reluctance to be both honest and vulnerable. The evangelical community has created an image of Christian maturity that no one can possibly attain. Acceptance and admiration are reserved for those who are better than most at camouflaging their sin and giving the appearance of having it all together. The result is a "church" more resembling a "religious country club" than a spiritual body of mutually dependent members.

Second, notwithstanding this sad state of affairs, God has called upon each of us to do whatever we can to heal people's hurts and to share their struggles. Only as we become deeply and directly involved in ministering to one another do we experience the sort of enriching fellowship and lasting relationships we read about in the Bible. There is a spiritual bonding that occurs among Christians only in the context of the mutual bearing of burdens.

Third, our failure to bear the burdens of others is largely due to ignorance, not only of the problems people experience but also of what it is about people that causes them to experience problems. We stand little chance of really helping one another so long as we remain ignorant of why people hurt.

Fourth, aside from the unavoidable difficulty and distress of living in a fallen world, most personal problems find their source in our fervent but often misdirected pursuit of love and purpose. How we behave in general and how we relate to others in particular is usually an expression of two factors: our sinful determination to find security and significance in someone or something other than Jesus Christ; and our manipulative efforts to protect ourselves from feelings of insecurity and insignificance when the people on whom we have depended fail us.

So where do we go from here? What steps should we take to help ease each other's burdens? Where do we focus our energies in our desire to minister and to be merciful to those who are hurting and alone and downcast and afraid? I hope to answer those questions in this chapter. But where do we begin?

SOLUTIONS THAT DON'T SOLVE

Some people would suggest that we need to start by dealing with our emotions. After all, one of the first things a struggling person will say is "I feel rotten," or, "I'm so mad I could spit," or, "I'm so low I have to reach up to touch bottom!" Few things in life are as real and vital and explosive as the emotions we experience.

No matter what the problem may be, people want to feel better, right now! Nothing seems more important than ridding ourselves of feelings that hurt and replacing them with whatever soothes and satisfies. And since we are all by nature suckers for the quick fix, we jump at the first word of counsel that promises pleasure in place of pain.

Larry Crabb tells of counseling a man who began the session

with the urgent request: "I want to feel better quick!" After a brief pause, Crabb replied: "I suggest you get a case of your favorite alcoholic beverage, find some cooperative women, and go to the Bahamas for a month."[1]

Needless to say, the man wondered aloud at whether Crabb had given him "biblical" advice. So Crabb proceeded to explain his answer: "It's the best I can do given your request. If you really want to feel good right away and get rid of any unpleasant emotion, then I don't recommend following Christ."[2] Was Christ the answer to this man's problem? Of course! But the man's problem was not that he was feeling bad. It obviously went much deeper.

Don't get me wrong. I'm not saying that feeling good is bad. Feeling good is great! But if emotion is the primary focus of our efforts to change (whether ourselves or others), the change will last only so long as the emotion does. (Or until the wine runs out and the women go home!) Feelings are notoriously fleeting. They come and go, rise and fall, with the circumstances of each passing day.

Supplying the downcast with a chemical stimulant or telling a resentful man to vent his anger by punching a pillow may provide short-term relief. But little has been done to deal with the root problem. *Unpleasant emotions are the consequences of our problems, not the cause.*

I will never forget the excruciating pain I felt in my left knee following the first day of football practice my freshman year in high school. An ice-pack and several aspirin later I felt great. But once the ice had melted and the medicine had run its course, the pain returned. You don't treat torn cartilage with an ice-pack and aspirin. Although knee surgery is quite painful, that's what the situation calls for.

The same principle applies to emotional pain. Whether it is torn cartilage or spiritual cancer, the surgery must be performed. Anything less will ultimately be both spurious and short-lived.

When I first began my counseling ministry, I would often experience feelings of utter failure when someone would leave without smiling. In most cases they had sought out my help because they were depressed or angry or bitter. In my naïveté I felt obligated to say or do something that would immediately lift their spirits. I soon realized that in most instances pain has to intensify before it can be relieved.

Well, then, maybe the problem lies in the circumstances of life. If the cause of a person's distress is the failure to achieve whatever goals he or she believes are essential to finding security and significance (see chapter 5), then identify the reason for the failure and change it. At least that's what many people would say. What we need, so they tell us, is a strategy for developing more effective methods to overcome those obstacles which prevent us from reaching our goals. If nothing else, this approach explains the flood of "How To" books in today's market.

I certainly have no inherent objection to learning *how to* do something more effectively. There is nothing evil or unbiblical in trying our best to improve the circumstances that confront us each day. Often those circumstances *are* responsible for hindering us from achieving our goals. If the goal in view is biblical, and if the circumstances are reasonably within your control, then go ahead and do what you can to change them. But don't be misled into thinking that altering your circumstances is some sort of panacea for all your problems.

Changing our circumstances, in this regard, is a lot like changing our emotions. It may provide some temporary relief, but in most cases the problem is too deep and complex to be solved by simply switching jobs or moving to another town or avoiding some person who is especially exasperating. As we are going to see, the real issue is not so much what your circumstances happen to be or the nature of the obstacles you encounter in pursuit of your goals, but rather how you *react* to them and why.

Let's not be fooled into thinking that our problems are ultimately traceable to people we don't like (or who don't like us) or places we don't want to live or any such external factor. The problem is on the inside. We've got to dig deeper than simply changing the outward course of events in our world.

When I shared these thoughts with a friend he was defiant in his response. He was convinced that the strain on his marriage was due to his wife's family. Their callous refusal to accept him or to appreciate his efforts to be a good husband was the cause of his misery.

Without wanting to diminish or deny the failure of his in-laws, I tried to persuade him that the source of the problem was more deeply-rooted. He wasn't inclined to listen. As far as he was concerned, packing his bags and moving out of state was the only way to resolve the conflict. He did, but it didn't!

Then, of course, if neither elevating our emotions nor changing our circumstances eases our pain, we can always blame it on sin! Just identify the rebellious behavior, confess it to the Lord, and then don't do it anymore! Resolve to do better next time; redouble your efforts to succeed.

Of course there's an element of truth in this approach as well. It *is* sinful to be angry without cause, or to feel bitter and resentful toward a neighbor, or to experience jealousy or hatred or uncontrolled lust or crippling anxiety. It *is* essential to acknowledge our transgressions before the Lord, and to rededicate ourselves, by His enabling grace, to live and feel as the Bible says we should. All this is absolutely necessary. But is it absolutely sufficient? I don't think so.

Simply knowing that I am wrongfully angry with my wife is one thing. Knowing *why* is something else. When I say knowing "why" I don't mean "because she messed up the checkbook again," or "because she criticized my best efforts." We've got to probe deeper than that. Otherwise we are back to blaming our problems on circumstances and obstacles of a merely external nature.

We must come to grips with *why* feelings of resentment well up within us when a close friend ignores us in favor of a rival. We must wrestle honestly with *why* we angrily withdraw from our mate when he or she treats us with calloused indifference. It isn't enough to say that such reactions are sinful. Of course they are. But I want to know why we commit such sin. What is it about who we are and how we think that prompts us to respond and relate to others in sinful ways?

The root cause of such reactions goes back to what we discovered in chapter 3: We long in the depth of our being for security in relationship with others and significance in the things we do.

These are not sinful desires, and we ignore them to the peril of our souls. God created us with these longings. He intends for us to seek to satisfy them in Him.

A REAL SOLUTION FOR REAL PROBLEMS

It would seem that we are now left with only one course of action. I have argued that most difficulties arise when we fail to reach those unbiblical goals on which we believe our security (love) and significance (purpose) depend, and then in turn manipulate others to protect our wounded hearts from any additional pain caused by feelings of insecurity and insignificance.

If this is the case, why don't we just change our goals? That's an excellent idea, but we need to remember that the goals we set are merely a reflection of what we believe will bring us personal fulfillment. Let me again explain what I mean.

A teenager sets a goal of academic excellence, believing that the love of his parents (security) is dependent upon it. A socialite strives to appear fashionable and chic, believing that her worth as a person (significance) hinges upon the approval of her social peers. Our goals, in other words, are an expression of our beliefs.

This is what I referred to earlier as the sin of misplaced dependency. We depend on everything except Jesus Christ to do what only He can do. Deeply embedded within our mental and emotional makeup are beliefs or assumptions concerning what will and will not quench the thirst of our souls. Real change, both in ourselves and in others, is possible only by ridding the human heart of the belief that it needs anything other than Christ to satisfy the hunger for security and significance.

So long as we believe that people or power or fame or fortune are essential for personal fulfillment, we shall continue to rely upon them in sinful independence of Christ. And so long as we depend on people and things to do what only Christ can do, we shall continue to manipulate and distort those people and things to protect ourselves from the pain of rejection and shattered expectations they will inevitably inflict.

Once we realize that only in a saving relationship with Christ can true security and significance be found, our goals will be gradually transformed. To obey Christ, to live in conformity with His revealed will, to seek His glory, becomes the aim of all we do and say. This kind of goal frees us from parasitic dependence upon others. It is a goal that cannot be frustrated by the sinful unreliability of those whose acceptance we thought we needed. It is a goal that fosters dependence on Christ alone, thereby *liberating us from a destructive and manipulative reliance on others.* We no longer demand of them that they do for us what they are incapable of doing.

You may still desire to be loved by others, accepted by a certain social group, recognized and praised for your efforts, and there is certainly nothing wrong with that. But you no longer *need* it. You may well suffer legitimate and understandable pain when your mate is inconsiderate and cold. There may be missing in your relationship with your spouse something glorious and great that God intends for a husband and wife. But that spouse's failure to provide you with the love you desire is no threat to your ultimate security.

In the case of one lady I have worked with, it took months before she abandoned her manipulative efforts to change her husband. She had vigorously insisted that happiness was possible . . . if only he would change! All that she asked was that he treat her with the sensitivity, tenderness, and understanding that her soul craved. She was astounded at the joy she felt once she finally gave up her sinful scheming.

This woman's willingness to terminate what she now acknowledges was selfish manipulation came with the growing realization that the Lord Jesus alone could (and would!) fulfill the deepest desires of her heart. Only after she realized that her security was dependent on *His* love, which can never fail, was she freed from depending on her husband to do what he either could not or would not do. She was now willing to risk ministering to him, not because *he* would never again reject her . . . but because *Christ* would not!

She still longs for her husband to change. And rightly she should. She still prays fervently for his renewal. So must we all. The difference now is . . . she doesn't *need* it.

Here is where the ministry of mercy must begin. This is the

first step down the path to genuine, lasting change. You may not be a gifted teacher or intellectual giant, but this ministry requires only a willing heart. It may not seem like much, but it's a start.

If you do nothing else, set your aim and focus your energy on exposing to your friend her misguided beliefs about where security and significance may be found. Help her to acknowledge how sinfully dependent she has become on things and people other than Christ to satisfy the thirst of her soul. Reveal to her (and to yourself, in your own struggles) the rebellious commitment of the human heart to make life work apart from reliance upon God. No real change will occur until each of us honestly (and painfully) acknowledges how thoroughly influenced our life has been by false and unbiblical beliefs. Larry Crabb puts it bluntly: "We must change our mind about the best way to deal with our thirsty soul."[3]

What we are talking about is what Paul had in view when he spoke of *renewing* our minds. In a verse most Christians know by heart, the apostle said it simply: "Do not conform any longer to the pattern of this world, but be transformed by the renewing of your mind" (Romans 12:2). This transformation, this change, comes when our *minds* (our beliefs) are renewed, *not* our emotions, circumstances, husband, wife, kids, job, friends, or salary. All else may stay the same, opposing and oppressing us. But if our minds, our beliefs, are being renewed, if we are deepening in our dependence on Christ for the satisfaction of our most urgent needs, we can withstand anything.

At the risk of oversimplification, what I am saying can be summed up in this way. In bearing the burdens of others, before you do anything else, strive by God's grace to persuade them of this paramount truth: *Whereas a lot of things in this world are nice, only Jesus Christ is necessary. Better still, He is enough!*

THE POISON OF SELF-PROTECTION

But there is one more thing that needs to be said. It isn't enough merely to experience a renewal in our minds. There must also be repentance in our hearts. Repentance from what, you ask?

Repentance from the sin of self-protection. Let me explain what this means.

No matter how thoroughly transformed our minds may be, there is still in each of us the pain of disappointment and rejection inflicted by those to whom we were looking for the fulfillment. "Dependency on others for the deep satisfaction that only God can provide," says Crabb, "is painful."[4]

Friends and family let us down, and it hurts. We don't like to admit it, lest we appear weak and vulnerable. But the pain is undeniably present. And the first priority of someone who has been hurt is to do whatever it takes to make sure it doesn't happen again. That is why "the beliefs we accept are more than a reflection of the ideas we were taught; they are carefully crafted efforts to lay out a strategy for minimizing pain and gaining whatever satisfaction can be found."[5]

So what can we do? We develop patterns of relating to others which are designed to protect ourselves from ever again experiencing the emotional agony of rejection and disappointment. These strategies, writes Crabb,

> essentially consist of interpersonal styles of relating that help us to achieve what we want: a level of *distance* from others that ensures invulnerability to further hurt, and a level of *contact* that allows others to touch us in ways that feel good. The balance is difficult to maintain: close enough to be affirmed, but far enough away to run little risk of serious hurt.[6]

We are all victims of failed relationships. We have all been disappointed and let down. And much of what we are today is the fruit of a carefully crafted agenda to cope with the pain of the past. We are determined not only to stay close enough to get the love we still desire, but also to keep far enough away to numb the pain we've already felt.

Thus our motivation in relating to others is at heart self-serving and therefore manipulative. We like to think we have the other person's best interests in mind. But all too often we treat them in whatever way we are convinced will prove most effective in protecting our own wounded souls from any further damage. Perhaps an illustration will help.

One summer in a softball game, the competitive drive got the better of me. As I slid into second base to avoid the tag, I suffered a posterior dislocation of my left shoulder. The pain was intense as I immediately popped it back into place. (Oh yes, for those of you who care to know, I was safe—even though the umpire didn't see it that way!) That little mishap put an end to my softball career, at least for one summer. My attention turned to one thing: Soothing the agony in my shoulder and making sure that no additional damage was inflicted. Everything I did, from the way I sat to the way I slept was geared toward one end: Protecting myself from any more pain.

Are we not much the same when it comes to protecting ourselves from emotional and spiritual injuries? When we are hurt, when the anguish of disappointment and rejection strike deeply within our souls, only one thing matters: Making sure we don't get hurt again. I don't slide into second base (or, for that matter, into any other base) anymore. My goal is to protect myself from suffering, and if it means being tagged out, so be it.

When we experience pain in our heart, our goal is no different. The moment we feel the distress of a broken relationship or shattered expectations, we instinctively do whatever is necessary to prevent it ever happening again.

The emotional and psychological pain that comes from being rejected by the person whose love you most deeply cherish is immeasurably more intense than that of a dislocated shoulder. As I write this chapter, my shoulder is almost as good as new. It rarely hurts anymore. But the wounds inflicted by rejection and scorn do not heal as quickly, and sometimes not at all.

When our work goes unappreciated, or is subjected to ridicule, the inner ache can be almost unbearable. The feeling of inferiority (or insignificance) is not a psychological "complex" experienced by only a few mentally unstable people. Virtually all of us have at some time or another endured the agony it produces. And our first reaction is to take steps to see that it won't recur.

James Dobson believes that "a sizable proportion of all human activity is devoted to the task of shielding us from the inner pain of inferiority."[7] He even goes so far as to suggest that this is "*the* most dominant force in life, even exceeding the power of sex in its influence."[8] I am inclined to agree. To think (usually wrongly) that those who know us the best may care for us the least cuts deeply into our hearts. To think that our best efforts will never be enough, is similarly painful.

The response to rejection differs from person to person, but the intent is usually the same. Some adopt an aggressive and brash style of relating. Others withdraw shyly, reluctant to express an opinion. Some become coldly efficient while still others give sacrificially of themselves beyond all reasonable limits. "Although natural differences account for much of our interpersonal style," argues Crabb, "beneath every method of relating can be found a commitment to self-interest, a determination to protect oneself from more relational pain."[9]

Not until we repent of that quest for self-protection, and are willing to risk being hurt yet again for the sake of the other person, shall we experience the quality change that the Bible calls Christian maturity.

It isn't easy to abandon self-protection in order to give oneself to and for another. It's risky. We've already suffered the pain it can yield and we don't want any more. The only way to overcome the fear that inhibits us from giving ourselves in loving ministry to those who cannot be trusted is to trust Someone else. We will never be willing to make ourselves truly vulnerable to others until we know how truly *in*vulnerable we are in Christ. We will never be willing to experience the rejection of those to whom we minister until we know how unconditional our acceptance is with the Lord Jesus.

The bottom line is this. There must be a renewal in our minds, a transformation of our beliefs as to *who is* truly able to quench the thirst of our souls. Christ alone can provide us with the security and significance we so desperately need. There must also be repentance in our heart, a turning from self-protection to risky involvement in the lives of others. Christ alone can be trusted never to hurt us. This is the beginning of change. This is how the burdens begin to lighten. This is the beginning of mercy.

SEVEN

Is Jesus Really Enough?

January 5, 1976, was a day that neither I nor my wife will soon forget. It was the dead of winter in Dallas, Texas, and as the sun set the temperature plummeted to well below the freezing mark. I was in my third year of seminary studies and, as was the case virtually every night, was up late reading.

"Fire!" The word rang out on that cold night with frightening urgency, bringing me out of my chair and into the parking lot of our apartment complex. There it was. Only three doors away a fire was raging. We later learned that a woman had become enraged with her husband and decided to seek vengeance. She piled all his clothes in the middle of the living room floor, doused them with lighter fluid, and set them aflame. She then sat down on the curb across from her apartment to watch.

My first reaction was to awaken Ann and get her to safety. By the time she had escaped and we had moved our car away from danger, the fire department arrived and cordoned off the entire complex. In doing so they shattered any hope I had of rushing back inside to save something of our possessions.

It was there in the parking lot at 11:00 p.m., in sub-freezing cold, that I learned an important lesson about myself. The flames did more than simply light up the cold Texas sky. They shone ablaze in my heart as well, dispelling the darkness of sin's deceit. While mournfully contemplating what would surely be the loss of all earthly possessions, it suddenly struck me how attached I had become to material things. My sinful dependence on earthly goods was exposed as I envisioned a future without clothes, without furniture, and worst of all, without theology books. I was shamed by the painful realization that my happiness was so closely tied up with what I owned.

Something our Lord said in the Sermon on the Mount quickly came to mind:

> "Do not store up for yourselves treasures on earth, where moth and rust [and fire!] destroy, and where thieves break in and steal. But store up for yourselves treasures in heaven, where moth and rust do not destroy, and where thieves do not break in and steal. For where your treasure is, there your heart will be also." (Matthew 6:19-21)

We frequently talk about Christ being all-sufficient, but I fear that it has become little more than a theological cliché. Though I had often affirmed this truth, I never really knew that Jesus was enough, until He was all that I had left. To be sure, I had my health; and my wife was safe. But in one chilling moment in 1976 it suddenly clicked: Jesus is not only necessary, He is enough.

As things turned out, the fire was extinguished just as it reached our apartment. There was extensive smoke and water damage, but most of our possessions (meager though they be) were saved. Still, the lesson I learned has stayed with me. If I have Christ, I have all I need. No material loss or personal tragedy, however painful or inconvenient it may be, can pose a threat to who I am and what I have in Christ. This is the simple but foundational truth on which all I have said in the previous chapters is based.

To this point we have been primarily concerned with the question, "Where do problems begin, and why?" I am persuaded that they are conceived and born in the sinful belief, embedded deeply within, that something or someone other than Jesus Christ can quench the thirst of our souls. Each of us by nature is determined to make life work without Christ. We are committed to independence at any cost.

Saint Augustine was the first to speak of a place in every heart that only God Himself can fill—a God-shaped vacuum. But we steadfastly refuse to believe it is true. We fervently try to stuff that vacuum with anything that will make us feel full. But like a Chinese dinner, though satisfying at first, soon we sense the gnawing hunger within.

The Lord Jesus Christ has invited us to feast to our everlasting fill and to drink of water that will forever quench our spiritually parched souls. But we persist in eating fast food and slaking our thirst at the shallow wells of a fallen world. Our sinful flesh refuses to feed on Christ, leaving us painfully empty and ever more determined to find satisfaction somewhere or in someone else.

CONTENTMENT IN CHRIST

In thinking along these lines I have often found both encouragement and insight in something Paul said in his letter to the Philippians. Having received a sizable monetary gift from these believers, Paul wrote them a thank-you note:

> I rejoice greatly in the Lord that at last you have renewed your concern for me. Indeed, you have been concerned, but you had no opportunity to show it. I am not saying this because I am in need, for I have learned to be content whatever the circumstances. I know what it is to be in need, and I know what it is to have plenty. I have learned the secret of being content in any and every situation, whether well fed or hungry, whether living in plenty or in want. I can do everything through him who gives me strength. (Philippians 4:10-13)

For some unexplained reason the Philippians had been temporarily unable to help Paul as they had at the beginning. It certainly wasn't for lack of desire. We shouldn't take Paul's words "at last" as if he meant, somewhat indignantly, "it's about time!" Evidently circumstances *beyond their control* had prevented these believers from supporting the apostle's work.

Although winter in Dallas is usually mild in comparison with other parts of the country, on occasion it can be quite severe. That was especially true in 1983 when an ice storm of unprecedented proportions struck the southwest. I was absolutely convinced that a sweet-gum tree in our front yard had become one of its victims. It looked as dead as can be. But Ann assured me over and over again that it was very much alive. "Give it time," she said. Sure enough, with the coming of spring, its leaves budded as the signs of life returned.

This is what Paul is saying about the Philippians and their concern for him. Indeed, the word translated "renewed" in verse 10, although used only here in the New Testament, elsewhere refers to the blossoming forth of a flower or tree after a long and cold winter freeze. Much in the way that Ann and I rejoiced over the signs of spring, so Paul rejoiced to see the resurgence of concern from Philippi after so long a period of silence. These believers had been like a tree, barren during the winter, but now alive and yielding its fruit.

Paul is also quick to realize that his exuberance might be misunderstood. Perhaps someone would interpret his joy upon receiving their gift as a sign of immaturity, like a child who has been given a new toy. He certainly didn't want them to think that his joy was stirred by the money itself. There might even have been some who would take his response as a veiled request for more! Knowing this, Paul quickly proceeds to declare that his happiness is independent of the gift itself. Neither prosperity nor poverty has any bearing on the emotional state of his soul.

He says, "for I have learned to be content whatever the circumstances" (verse 11). Every time I see the word *content* I can't help but recall the commercial for a particular brand of milk. Do you remember their claim? "Our milk comes from 'contented' cows!" What in the world does a contented cow look like? Or for that matter, a discontented one? Can you imagine Old MacDonald reporting to his wife, "Honey, we've got problems. Our cows aren't contented!"

So what does it mean to be "contented"? What is Paul saying when he tells us that he has learned to be "content" in the midst of any and all circumstances? It helps again to look at the word he uses. This particular term was a favorite one among the Stoics, those ancient philosophers who prided themselves on living independently of the world around them. Whatever resources were necessary for survival came from within, as they disciplined themselves to shun any reliance on external aids or props. They looked neither to people nor possessions, living virtually unaffected by the world around them.

Being a Dallas Cowboys fan, I can't help but laugh when people describe the team's first and now former coach, Tom Landry. Mr. Landry is not only a remarkable coach but a faithful Christian as well. His placid and stone-faced demeanor during even the most exciting and crucial games has prompted many to describe him as "stoical." The suggestion is that he lives above and beyond the reach of the emotions of the game. There's an element of truth here. Though Landry passionately wants to win, a loss (or several in a row, as was the case in his last year with the team) poses no personal threat—and it shows in his face.

I'm not at all suggesting that Paul was a stone-faced apostle, or in any way reluctant to display his feelings. But something about this man of God enabled him to experience a spiritual contentment in the midst of indescribably tumultuous and often tragic circumstances. In his second letter to the church at Corinth he briefly described what his ministry for the sake of the gospel had entailed:

> I have worked much harder, been in prison more frequently, been flogged more severely, and been exposed to death again and again. Five times I received from the Jews the forty lashes minus one. Three times I was beaten with rods, once I was stoned, three times I was shipwrecked, I spent a night and a day in the open sea, I have been constantly on the move. I have been in danger from rivers, in danger from bandits, in danger from my own countrymen, in danger from Gentiles; in danger in the city, in danger in the country, in danger at sea; and in danger from false brothers. I have labored and toiled and have often gone without sleep; I have known hunger and thirst and have often gone without food; I have been cold and naked. (2 Corinthians 11:23-27)

Without in any way minimizing your problems, how do your struggles compare with Paul's? Yet he dares to tell us that he has "learned to be *content* whatever the circumstances." This ability was not something Paul was born with. *It had to be learned.* It was evidently the result of a long and painful process during which Paul somehow weaned himself from reliance on anything or anyone.

"I know what it is to be in need," he says. "I know what it means to go to bed hungry. I know what it is to have friends turn their back on you in an hour of desperate need" (see 2 Timothy 1:15, 4:9-18). I also "know what it is to have plenty. I know how to be abased and yet not crushed by it. There have even been times of relative abundance, but I am careful not to let myself be unduly exalted or in any way become smug with success," says Paul. "I have learned how to fight depression when I lack the luxuries of life. And when I'm healthy and free, I resist the temptation to become puffed up with pride and self-satisfaction."

He seems to be saying, "My happiness and joy transcend bodily hurts or health, poverty or prosperity, the turbulent as well as the tranquil. I can face each day poor and hungry while maintaining my spiritual and emotional equilibrium. I can fall asleep filled and prosperous without losing sight of the God from whom all good gifts ultimately come. I know how to be deprived of material blessings and peaceful surroundings without thinking that life has lost its purpose. And I know how to thrive and feel good without being deceived into thinking that such pleasure alone is what makes life worth living."

None of this suggests that Paul was some sort of first century Mr. Spock, the Vulcan from Star Trek who lived by logic, devoid of genuine human emotion and passion. No one can read Paul's epistles or the story of his life in the book of Acts and deny that he was a man of great emotional warmth and depth.

Paul was capable not only of righteous indignation and rage, but also of a love profoundly sensitive to the needs of others. Perhaps Paul himself explained his contentment best when he said, "We are hard pressed on every side, but not crushed; perplexed, but not in despair; persecuted, but not abandoned; struck down, but not destroyed" (2 Corinthians 4:8-9).

Regarding Paul's apparent "stoicism," commentator Gerald Hawthorne observes that,

> the difference between Paul, the self-sufficient Christian, and the self-sufficient Stoic, is vast: "The self-sufficiency of the Christian is relative: an independence of the world through dependence upon God. The Stoic self-sufficiency pretends to be absolute. One is the contentment of faith, the other of pride. Cato and Paul both stand erect and fearless before a persecuting world: one with a look of rigid, defiant scorn; the other with a face now lighted up with unutterable joy in God."[1]

The secret Paul had learned was Christ! "I can do everything through him who gives me strength" (Philippians 4:13). The inner resource on which Paul would draw was not the power of the flesh but the power of the risen Lord. How did the apostle cope? Very simply by learning the lesson I hope and pray each of us learns: *that Jesus is enough!* "The secret of Paul's independence," says Hawthorne, "was his dependence upon Another. His self-sufficiency in reality came from being in vital union with One who is all-sufficient."[2] By God's grace Paul had made great strides in ridding himself of the sin of misplaced dependency. His dependency was placed in Christ.

THE BIBLICAL BOTTOM LINE

I don't think Paul could have been any more explicit than this. I don't think he needs to be. He offers no fancy formulas or complex theories. The bottom line is: Either you believe in the adequacy of Jesus Christ or you don't. Paul did. And it made all the difference in the world in how he dealt with defeat and rejection and how he coped with the frightening circumstances he faced.

There are, however, two sides to this truth. Some of us, like Paul, have to be weaned from self in order to learn dependency on God. But if Paul once suffered from too much confidence in his own abilities, Moses is an example of someone who suffered from too little. Both men had to learn that "all things" can indeed be accomplished, but only "through Him who gives us strength."

Moses was plagued by self-doubt. Stung by the memory of his impetuous murder of an Egyptian, he balked when God selected him to deliver the Jews from bondage. Self-doubt, to be sure, is not always bad. Neither, for that matter, is self-confidence. But self-doubt must lead to trust in God or it serves only to paralyze and inhibit. Self-doubt ought not produce despair, but should drive us to God from whom we draw the strength and skills that we ourselves lack.

Forty years had passed since Moses fled Egypt for Midian. Forty years of long, tedious tending of sheep and goats. Forty years in which Moses questioned himself and God. The time of deliverance for Israel finally came. Moses must have said to himself, *Surely God will deliver them by the power of angelic hosts or through a mighty army of the faithful.* What came next shook Moses down to his sandals: "So now, go. I am sending you to Pharaoh to bring my people the Israelites out of Egypt" (Exodus 3:10).

Moses' response is a mixture of self-doubt and genuine humility: "But Moses said to God, 'Who am I, that I should go to Pharaoh and bring the Israelites out of Egypt?' And God said, 'I will be with you'" (verses 11-12). Clearly Moses had missed the point entirely. He asks "Who am I?" But *who Moses is* isn't the issue. *Who God is* is what matters. It isn't Moses, but who is with Moses that will make the difference.

We often find ourselves confronted with tasks of far less significance than either Moses or Paul, yet we persistently ask, "Who am I, Lord?" To be honest, the answer may well be: "Not much!" The fact is, we *are* too weak and impetuous and ill-prepared, by ourselves, to do anything of lasting importance for God. But that's okay. *God wants it that way.* It is as if God had said to Moses, "If you really were somebody, you might get the glory when the Israelites are delivered. But because you are an inarticulate and impetuous shepherd, I, Yahweh, will get all the glory." And that's how it should be.

Paul stressed this theme in 1 Corinthians 1:26-29, in speaking of God's purpose in divine election:

> Brothers, think of what you were when you were called. Not many of you were wise by human standards; not many were influential; not many were of noble birth. But God chose the

> foolish things of the world to shame the wise; God chose the weak things of the world to shame the strong. He chose the lowly things of this world and the despised things—and the things that are not—to nullify the things that are, so that no one may boast before him.

The disciples must have felt much like Moses as they heard the Lord Jesus issue His Great Commission (Matthew 28:18-20). Going into all the world and discipling the nations is a tall order, even for men like Peter and John. Some of these men probably had too much, and others too little confidence in themselves at the time they heard those words. Each of them, though, had to learn what Moses and Paul knew: Ultimately it is our great Triune God through whom we do all things. The disciples went forth in confidence, not because of who they were but because of who was with them: "And surely I am with you always, to the very end of the age" (verse 20).

Is Jesus enough? You may want me to say more than this. You may want Paul or Moses or some other biblical author to say more. After all, it's embarrassing to suddenly realize how simple the solution is. Sometimes we prefer to believe the answer is deep and profound, because that would give an excuse for not doing anything about our problems.

I have no desire to make light of your struggles. In saying the solution is simple I'm not chiding you for failing to understand what a child of ten could see. But how else can I say it? Paul's language won't permit me to put it in any other terms. It was true for him (and for Moses) and it is true for us: The secret to successful Christian living is the sufficiency of Christ! Period.

FAITH OR FEAR?

Take yourself in hand for a moment and ask some heart-probing questions. "Why do I not give myself wholly to Christ? Why do I balk at many of His commands? Why do I keep a tight emotional grip on material possessions, allowing them to cloud my commitment to Christ? Why do I keep silent when I know that God would have me share the gospel with an unsaved neighbor? Why do I vigorously defend myself when unjustly slandered?" I think the answer is obvious: Fear.

J. I. Packer offers some penetrating insights on this all-too-common problem among Christians:

> We shrink from accepting burdens of responsibility for others because we fear we should not have strength to bear them. We shrink from accepting a way of life in which we forfeit material security because we are afraid of being left stranded. We shrink from being meek because we are afraid that if we do not stand up for ourselves we shall be trodden down and victimized, and end up among life's casualties and failures. We shrink from breaking with social conventions in order to serve Christ because we fear that if we did, the established structure of our life would collapse all round us, leaving us without a footing anywhere.[3]

It isn't so much that we deliberately turn our backs on Christ's call to take up our cross and follow Him. It isn't that we don't love the Savior or that we are ungrateful for His multitude of blessings. What is lacking is simple faith that God is both willing and able to provide for the needs of those who risk everything in the pursuit of holiness.

Those of us who lack this faith are often the very people who have experienced betrayal by someone we deeply loved. Few things in life are more devastating than being left emotionally and physically stranded by the one person in whose love and commitment we placed our trust. If you have any doubts about this, ask the mother of three young children whose husband just left her for his secretary, or the seven-year-old girl whose father repeatedly abused her.

Human love is fickle. People are often painfully unreliable. And some make the tragic mistake of thinking that God is no better. But human failure is not the measure of divine fidelity. As difficult as it may be to again entrust yourself to the care of another, be assured that God is adequate. He is reliable. He will never, by no means ever, leave you or forsake you.

The bottom line, then, is that we fail to give and to serve and to sacrifice and to minister because we are fearful of being shortchanged. We are afraid that in attending to others we will be left unattended. We are afraid that our most urgent needs will go unmet, and the prospect of more disappointment and emotional pain is simply too horrifying to ignore. Our fears are fueled by the corroding doubt as to God's adequacy to do for us what will inevitably need to be done.

We must say it. We must confess it out loud. The primary reason we spend our lives in sinful and ultimately destructive dependency on other people, manipulating them to meet our needs, is because we do not believe that Christ can.

The primary reason we are wedded to our wealth is our belief that it can do what Christ can't. Listen again to the apostle: "If God is for us [you!], who can be against us [you!]? He who did not spare his own Son, but gave him up for us all [for you!]—how will he not also, along with him, graciously give us [you!] all things?" (Romans 8:31-32).

Is Paul saying that, had I lost all my possessions in the apartment fire, I would still have "all things"? Is he saying that, if my wife leaves me and my friends ridicule me and my career collapses, I would still have "all things"? Yes! Paul is telling us that no loss is ultimate, no impoverishment irreparable, *as long as we have Christ.*

The "all things" that come with Christ are not necessarily material blessings or physical health or any of those things we assume are essential for earthly contentment. Packer says that Paul's admonition,

> has to do with knowing and enjoying God, and not with anything else. The meaning of "He will give us all things" can be expressed thus: One day we shall see that nothing—literally nothing—which could have increased our eternal happiness has been denied us, and that nothing—literally nothing—that could have reduced that happiness has been left with us. What higher assurance do we want than that?[4]

A SYMPATHETIC SAVIOR

In her book *Glorious Intruder*, Joni Eareckson Tada tells the story of a thirteen-year-old girl named Kerrie. For some unexplained reason Kerrie has become the object of her classmates' scorn and ridicule. She is teased and tormented daily, yet offers no resistance.

What makes it so cruel, says Joni, "is the anguish this girl suffers. Deep pain and perplexity, smothered and suppressed, still shows in her eyes."[5] The question we ask is, "Does our Lord identify with that kind of suffering?"[6] Is He sufficient to meet the needs arising from the kind of pain no one sees?

We all know that Jesus suffered physically. We are all familiar with the details of His abuse at the hands of the Roman soldiers and His eventual execution on a cross. But Kerrie's suffering, perhaps like yours, is on the inside. What can Jesus possibly do about that?

Joni wisely points us to Isaiah 53 where we read of the pain Jesus endured daily. One of the first things we notice is that our Lord was probably not the most handsome guy in the ancient world. In verses 2-3 we are told, "He had no beauty or majesty to attract us to him, nothing in his appearance that we should desire him. He was despised and rejected by men, a man of sorrows, and familiar with suffering. Like one from whom men hide their faces he was despised, and we esteemed him not."

Evidently Jesus knew what it was like to be ignored. He knew what it was like to be laughed at. He knew the pain of loneliness and rejection that comes from being average-looking, or perhaps even downright unattractive.

In verse 6 Isaiah says, "We all, like sheep, have gone astray, each of us has turned to his own way; and the Lord has laid on him the iniquity of us all." Joni describes what Jesus must have felt:

> Everybody turned away from Him. Alone, Jesus shouldered the burden of our sin and rebellion. Just as you have felt the stab of other people's pity or the indifference of uncaring friends, Jesus, too, endured the sting of rebuff and the ache of loneliness. And it wasn't an occasional thing from a few

> fair-weather friends. He felt the awful realization that *no one* was on His side. No one bothered to listen or care.
>
> Verse 11 speaks of the "suffering of his soul." That has to be the worst kind of suffering possible . . . when you cry those deep, heaving sobs that come from *way* down inside. Real anguish you just can't stop.
>
> You know how that feels. So does He.[7]

That's really the message of this chapter: Jesus does understand the ache on the inside, having felt it in His own soul to a depth far beyond what you or I will ever know. Have you been ignored? So was He. Have your friends abandoned you? So did His. Have you been treated cheaply? So was He. That is why, says Joni, "if you bring that pain to Him, He will never make light of it."[8]

BROKEN ARM, BROKEN HEART

I was only six years old when I fell from the top of a fence and shattered my left elbow on the concrete base of a clothesline pole. Little boys break their arms all the time, but this proved to be far more serious than anyone could have anticipated.

After several days in a local hospital I was transferred to a larger and better-equipped facility in Oklahoma City. It has been almost thirty-five years ago, but the memory of that day has not faded in the least.

Private rooms simply were not available. I was placed in a ward with two dozen other kids my age. Neither my mother nor father were permitted to stay the night with me. When it came time to bid them good-night, I made one request. My father and I searched for a quiet place to be alone for a few minutes. We had to settle for the men's rest room. We looked around the corner and peeked into the stalls to make certain we were alone. I remember standing on top of the toilet seat with one arm in a cast and the other wrapped firmly around my dad's neck. His embrace almost squeezed the breath out of me, but I didn't mind. I got his shirt wet with tears, but he didn't seem to mind.

When he and my mother finally tore themselves away, I had

my first real taste of loneliness . . . and it was bitter. I was surrounded by noise, but I was lonely. There were nurses at every turn, but I was lonely. The other kids in the ward were friendly, but I was lonely. I'm not ashamed to say I cried myself to sleep that night, and several nights thereafter.

But hear me well. The most horrifying cry of loneliness ever heard didn't come from an aged widow or a prisoner in solitary confinement or even from a frightened six-year-old boy with a broken arm. It came from a cross, from the lips of a sinless Savior named Jesus: "My God, my God, why have you forsaken me?" (Matthew 27:46).

So what's the point? Jesus knows who you are, where you are, and better still, He knows how you feel. When no one else is around, or even cares to be, Jesus is. You see, we never really know that Jesus is enough until He's all we've got left.

Max Lucado gets to the heart of what I'm trying to say:

> I keep thinking of all the people who cast despairing eyes toward the dark heavens and cry "Why?" And I imagine him [Jesus]. I imagine him listening. I picture his eyes misting and a pierced hand brushing away a tear. And although he may offer no answer, although he may solve no dilemma, although the question may freeze painfully in mid-air, he who also was once alone, understands.[9]

If you and I learn nothing else, if this book leaves us with but one thought, let it be that in Jesus Christ we have a truly sympathetic Savior . . . one who knows our pain and can meet the need of any moment, however agonizing it may be.

We can take the risk of loving those on whose response we cannot depend, because we are accepted in the Beloved. We can take the risk of vulnerable ministry to those who cannot be trusted, because Christ can be trusted! We can give without hope of return, we can serve without hope of being served, knowing we are secure in Christ's love and are of immeasurable value to His heart.

EIGHT

An Ordinary Man and His Extraordinary Love

I've already confessed to being a mechanical idiot (chapter 5), so I might as well come clean about something else. I'm an incurable, unrepentant romantic. It's probably best that I not go into detail about this, other than to say that my all-time favorite movie is *Camelot*, starring Richard Harris (King Arthur) and Vanessa Redgrave (Guinevere).

Only a true romantic would rate *Camelot* above such classics of the cinema as *Gone with the Wind*, *Citizen Kane*, and *The Godfather*. Only a true romantic would acknowledge that his favorite song in the movie is, "How to Handle a Woman." Confused by Guinevere's behavior, Arthur wonders aloud in song:

How to handle a woman,
There's a way, said the wise old man;
A way known by every woman,
Since the whole rigmarole began.

Do I flatter her? I begged him answer.
Do I threaten, cajole, or plead?
Do I brood, play the game, romance her?
Said he, smiling, No indeed.

How to handle a woman,
Mark me well, I will tell you sir.

The way to handle a woman,
Is to love her,
Simply love her,
Merely love her,
Love her,
Love her.[1]

Every time I hear Richard Harris sing this song (and yes, I do continue to watch the movie on video cassette), I wonder if it is really as easy as he makes it sound. (You would think that after nineteen years of marriage I would know!) *Simply* love her? *Merely* love her? Feminists will undoubtedly accuse me of being a chauvinist, but I think King Arthur has a point. After all, when the Apostle Paul gave instructions to husbands on how to relate to their wives, he summed up by saying, "Husbands, *love* your wives, just as Christ loved the Church and gave himself up for her" (Ephesians 5:25, emphasis added). If husbands were to love their wives to the extent and with the fervency that Christ loved *His* bride, the Church, little more would be necessary. Such is the profoundly powerful effect of Christlike love.

The same holds true in our relationships with other believers. I seriously doubt this book would have been written had Christians loved one another as the Bible tells them to. I'm not trying to be flippant or simplistic. There's an obvious risk in urging Christians *simply* and *merely* to love one another. But sadly, *love* is a word which in today's world either means absolutely nothing or virtually anything.

But the modern abuse of the term does not absolve you and me from heeding the biblical exhortation. If you think I'm trivializing a complex issue I can only ask that you reconsider what the Holy Spirit had in mind when He inspired the biblical authors to employ the word love. As I have come to understand the biblical love ethic, it is anything but trivial. Its demands are far-reaching and its effects are revolutionary. So, if I may be permitted to paraphrase King Arthur's song:

How to bear someone's burdens,
Mark me well, I will tell you sir.

The way to bear someone's burdens,
Is to love her,
Simply love him,
Merely love them,
Love them,
Love them.

LOVE IN ACTION

Some things are best explained, not with a definition but with an example. Nowhere is this more true than in considering our responsibility and privilege to love others with Christlike love. The person I have in mind who embodies Christian love is a most unlikely figure. He's really quite ordinary. You realize, I am sure, that I'm taking a risk in not using a famous name to illustrate the point of this chapter. In today's world if you want to sell a product or push legislation or increase the percentage share of television ratings, a real celebrity is essential. Someone from Hollywood or the National Football League will do just fine.

Christians are not immune to the glamorous appeal of the highly successful and well-known actress or athlete. That is why we sit up and take notice when a biblical celebrity is mentioned; someone like Abraham or Moses or David or Paul or John. But not this time. I want us to look at love in the life of an average layman, a man whose name few have heard and even fewer remember. I'm talking about Epaphroditus.

"Remember it? I can't even pronounce it," is a typical response when I mention this man's name. It is an unusual name. It is derived from the name of Aphrodite, the Greek goddess of love (that's convenient!). Some have suggested that the parents of Epaphroditus were pagan devotees of the goddess, but we have no way of knowing this. What is important, and obvious, is that although his name was of pagan origin his heart belonged to the Lord Jesus Christ. Here is what Paul said of him:

> But I think it is necessary to send back to you Epaphroditus, my brother, fellow worker and fellow soldier, who is also your messenger, whom you sent to take care of my needs.

> For he longs for all of you and is distressed because you heard he was ill. Indeed he was ill, and almost died. But God had mercy on him, and not on him only but also on me, to spare me sorrow upon sorrow. Therefore I am all the more eager to send him, so that when you see him again you may be glad and I may have less anxiety. Welcome him in the Lord with great joy, and honor men like him, because he almost died for the work of Christ, risking his life to make up for the help you could not give me. (Philippians 2:25-30)

At first glance Paul's personal comments about Epaphroditus in verses 25-30 (and about Timothy in verses 19-24) seem out of place. He usually reserves this sort of thing for the conclusion of his letters. So why here? The answer is found in what Paul had said a few verses earlier in chapter 2.

The most famous passage in Philippians is the "Christ Hymn" in 2:6-11. There Paul appealed to the self-sacrificial, voluntary humiliation of Christ as the model of how we ought to behave toward one another in the Church. "Do nothing out of selfish ambition or vain conceit," said Paul, "but in humility consider others better than yourselves. Each of you should look not only to your own interests, but also to the interests of others" (2:3-4).

This is the attitude or frame of mind that Jesus had (verses 6-11) and that we should have as well (verse 5). This is certainly how Paul conducted himself (verse 17). So also did Timothy and Epaphroditus. Paul mentions them here, rather than in his customary closing remarks, to provide his readers with two living examples of what it means to lovingly seek the interests of others, even as Christ Jesus did.

So what had Epaphroditus done? Evidently he had served as an emissary or envoy of the church at Philippi in bringing to Paul a substantial financial gift (see 1:4-5, and especially 4:14-19). He then had remained in Rome and ministered to Paul as a personal aide. During the course of his tenure there, Epaphroditus fell ill, almost died, was eventually healed, and is now being sent back to Philippi bearing in hand this epistle.

In his book *Liberating Ministry from the Success Syndrome*, Kent Hughes retells a fourth-century story of the difficulty some inexperienced demons were finding in their effort to tempt a godly hermit. They used everything at their disposal, but to no avail.

> Frustrated, the imps returned to Satan and recited their plight. He responded that they had been far *too hard* on the monk. "Send him a message," he said, "that his brother has just been made bishop of Antioch. Bring him *good* news." Mystified by the devil's advice, the demons nevertheless returned and dutifully reported the wonderful news to the hermit. And, in that very instant, he fell—into deep, wicked jealousy.[2]

Neither Paul nor Epaphroditus suffered from this sort of professional jealousy, which so often infects even Christian coworkers. It would have been easy for Paul to look down his apostolic nose on someone like Epaphroditus, or for Epaphroditus to ache with envy as he reflected on the success of Paul's ministry. In a moment we will see how selfless and giving Epaphroditus was, but for now let's take note of Paul.

Here was an apostle, one of only a handful of men who had seen the resurrected and exalted Christ. He was a brilliant theologian and spiritually gifted beyond most in the early Church, perfect soil in which the seeds of arrogance and conceit might grow. Yet Paul looked on Epaphroditus and saw a "brother," a "fellow worker," and a "fellow soldier." Many of us begrudge the gifts God has given to others, perhaps threatened by their success or fearful of our own loss of prestige. Paul can only praise Epaphroditus. He holds him in the highest esteem possible.

This man whom you sent to me, says Paul, has taken care of my needs (2:25). The word translated "take care of" ("minister" in the NASB) is *leitourgos*, from which we get *liturgy*. In the Greek translation of the the Old Testament Scriptures it often refers to the priestly and sacrificial duties of those who administer the sacred rites of the Levitical order. Epaphroditus, says Paul, in caring for me, was rendering a distinctly religious and priestly service. He was my minister!

Still, Paul felt obliged to send him back to Philippi, "for he longs for all of you and is distressed because you heard he was ill" (verse 26). Epaphroditus was homesick. More than that, he was just plain sick. But look carefully at what Paul says. It wasn't that Epaphroditus, being physically sick, was concerned for his own welfare. Strange as it may sound, his concern was for *their* concern once they heard of his illness. This is Christian love! Epaphroditus cared deeply for the Philippians, so much so that he was less concerned for his own physical health than he was for their emotional health once they learned of his affliction.

Most of us take the opportunity of personal illness to indulge in a little self-pity (sometimes a *lot*). We don't enjoy the physical pain and discomfort, but we can't keep ourselves from taking selfish satisfaction in the special attention others show us in our hour of need. But look at Epaphroditus. Here is a man who probably prayed more to God concerning the grief of his friends over his illness than he prayed to God for his own physical welfare.

Paul says Epaphroditus was "distressed" when he discovered that the Christians in his home church had received news of his illness. He couldn't bear the thought of being a burden to them, even if only in their minds. The word translated "distressed" is the one Mark uses to describe the emotional turmoil Jesus experienced in the Garden of Gethsemane (Mark 14:33). Far from feeling gratified that he was the object of so much conversation and prayerful concern back home, Epaphroditus was driven to mental torment that he, though by no fault of his own, had become a source of sorrow to them!

I don't want to dwell on Epaphroditus's illness except to point out its cause. Paul says, "He almost died for the work of Christ, risking his life to make up for the help you could not give me" (Philippians 2:30). Once again, Paul's choice of terms sheds light on Epaphroditus. The word translated "risking" is one that Paul himself may well have coined for the occasion. The idea behind it is of someone who has gambled or gone out on a limb in a particularly risky venture. From this word alone, suggests Gerald Hawthorne,

> It is clear that Epaphroditus was no coward, but a courageous person willing to take enormous risks, ready to play with very high stakes in order to come to the aid of a person in need. He did not "save" his life, but rather

hazarded it to do for Paul and for the cause of Christ what other Philippian Christians did not or could not do.[3]

Epaphroditus was willing to sacrifice everything in Christian love. His affection for Paul, and ultimately for Christ Jesus, was so intense that he took little regard for himself. When it came to bearing the burdens of the apostle, no risk was too great, no stakes too high.

Epaphroditus wasn't the sort of person who in today's world would win an Oscar nomination or the MVP trophy in the Super Bowl. There aren't too many sponsors who would hire him to sell their product; I even doubt that he would be asked to share his testimony on any of our Christian television talk-shows. He is hardly anyone's idea of a celebrity. But Paul says, "*Honor* men like him" (emphasis added). What had he done to merit such recognition from an apostle and an entire church? He had loved, and almost died doing it.

The authenticity of Epaphroditus's affection can hardly be doubted. Elsewhere Paul insists that "love must be sincere" (Romans 12:9, cf. 1 Peter 1:22). The word *sincere* translates the Greek term *anhupocritos*, the opposite of *hupocritos*, from which we get *hypocrisy*. This particular Greek term often appeared in the context of the ancient theater. One form of the word was used of a stage actor. Since performers in Greek drama frequently wore masks, the word came to suggest someone who cloaked his true feelings while putting on an outward show. This is the sort of person who merely acts, or somehow pretends to be someone he, in reality, is not.

Christian love, says Paul, must never be this way. Epaphroditus loved Paul and the Philippians with a single-minded sincerity. His was a genuine love, authentic in every respect. Jesus said, "As I have loved you, so you must love one another" (John 13:34). Epaphroditus did just that . . . and it almost killed him!

THE DYNAMICS OF CHRISTIAN LOVE

We are now ready to look at the dynamics of Christian love. We need to see what love *does*.

1. The Lord Jesus Christ loved the Philippians so much that He "made himself nothing . . . and became obedient to death—even death on a cross!" (Philippians 2:7-8). This is the immovable foundation and the life-giving source from which all other truths concerning Christian love must flow. As John said, "This is love: not that we loved God, but that he loved us and sent his Son as an atoning sacrifice for our sins. Dear friends, since God so loved us, we also ought to love one another" (1 John 4:10-11).
2. The Apostle Paul loved the Philippians so much that he endured a cruel beating and unjust imprisonment (Acts 16) to bring them the gospel and, as this letter attests, is deeply burdened by their struggles.
3. The Philippians loved Paul so much that they generously gave of their financial resources to support him in his missionary endeavors.
4. Epaphroditus loved Paul so much that he risked his life in ministering to his every need.
5. The Philippians loved Epaphroditus so much that they grieved upon receiving news of his illness.
6. Epaphroditus loved the Philippians so much that he grieved upon receiving news of their receiving news of his illness!
7. Finally, Paul loved Epaphroditus so much that he would have felt "sorrow upon sorrow" (Philippians 2:27) had his dear friend and coworker died.

WHAT DOES A CHRISTIAN LOOK LIKE?

None of this should surprise us. If it does, it only shows how far short we have fallen from the agenda Jesus set for His people. You will recall that it was on the eve of His crucifixion, sometime during the solemn observance of that last Passover meal with His disciples, that Jesus said, "By this all men will know that you are my disciples, if you love one another" (John 13:35).

We don't possess a photograph or even a verbal description of Epaphroditus. We have no way of knowing whether he was tall or short, handsome or homely. Odds are he was average looking, without any special physical features that might attract the attention of others. He didn't wear a clerical collar or don the elegant robes of a high church "Reverend."

Today it is easy to locate a devotee of Krishna. He's the bald-headed fellow with the tambourine. The Amish are readily known by their dress and the horse-drawn buggy. We are also quick to identify a Mormon missionary. The dark slacks, white shirt, and bicycle have become his trademark. But lacking such distinctive features, how would anyone have known Epaphroditus to be a Christian?

They wouldn't have known it because of his theological expertise, although I'm confident he could hold up his end of a conversation with Paul on any topic of interest. Nor was it because of some charismatic power to heal the sick, otherwise he would not have fallen ill himself. But I guarantee you one thing: Everyone knew Epaphroditus was a Christian. We have Christ's word on it!

Tertullian (AD 160–215) was one of the more illustrious and controversial among the early Church Fathers. Concerning the impact of the Christian community in his day on the pagan world, he is reported as saying: "But it is mainly the deeds of a love so noble that lead many to put a brand upon us. 'See,' they say, 'how they love one another!'"

Chrysostom (AD 344–407), on the other hand, lamented that Christians displayed so little love for each other that the world turned its back on the gospel: "Even now, there is nothing else that causes the heathen to stumble, except that there is no love [among us]. . . . Their own doctrines they have long condemned, and in like manner they admire ours, but they are hindered by our mode of life."

That is still true today. The beauty and truth of our doctrine notwithstanding, in the absence of love the unbeliever turns away. A few years ago I was stunned by a report that appeared on the local news concerning a prominent church in the community. A young couple with three children had been members for some time, supporting the church financially and serving it in other ways. Sadly, though, they had suffered numerous monetary and physical setbacks. Upon turning to the church leadership for assistance, they were rudely denied any supportive ministry. They had, purportedly, become an embarrassment to those in the congregation who espoused a gospel of prosperity and social sophistication.

It was not the *doctrine* of the church that evoked the curiosity of the local media. Quite frankly, they didn't know and couldn't have cared less what the church believed. But when it appeared they had failed to love their own, it suddenly became newsworthy.

If we today were without our ornate churches with huge auditoriums, stained-glass windows, and spacious balconies, how would an outsider know there were Christians in the community? If there were no ecclesiastical buildings of imposing architectural beauty, no choir lofts, no baptistries, how would the nonChristian tell the difference between us and the weekly gathering of some other civic organization? What is it about Christian people that sets them apart from nonChristians? Were we never to sing a hymn, pass an offering plate, or preach from God's Word, how would they know we were any different from them? "By this," said Jesus, "all men will know that you are my disciples, if you love one another." That's how.

So permit this self-confessed romantic to say it again:

How to bear someone's burdens,
Mark me well, I will tell you sir.
The way to bear someone's burdens,
Is to love her,
Simply love him,
Merely love them,
Love them,
Love them.

TO WHAT LENGTHS, LOVE?

There's one more question to answer: Just how far must our love go? How deep? How radical? How much does it require? Jesus answers the question for us, not with words, but with a touch of His hand. Matthew tells the story:

> When he came down from the mountainside, large crowds followed him. A man with leprosy came and knelt before him and said, "Lord, if you are willing, you can make me clean." Jesus reached out his hand, and touched the man. "I am willing," he said. "Be clean!" Immediately he was cured of his leprosy. (Matthew 8:1-3)

C. F. Weigle wrote both the lyrics and melody of one of my favorite hymns. You probably know it:

> No one ever cared for me like Jesus, There's no other friend so kind as He; No one else could take the sin and darkness from me, O how much He cared for me.[4]

Surely the man Jesus healed in Matthew 8 would have liked this song. "No one ever, *ever* cared for me like Jesus!" Remember, he was a *leper*. Few of us have ever seen leprosy except as it is portrayed in Hollywood movies. I'm sure we'd like to keep it that way. Leprosy doesn't make for the best dinner conversation. But we will never know the lengths to which our love must go until we understand something about leprosy. That may sound strange, but bear with me.

Leprosy begins with the discoloration of a patch of skin. In the more serious form of leprosy, lepromatous, it soon spreads widely in all directions. Spongy tumors swell up on the face and body, causing horrible disfigurement. The skin around the eyes and ears often begins to bunch up, with deep furrows between the swellings. The tissues between the bones of the hands and feet deteriorate, leaving fingers and toes badly deformed. It isn't uncommon for them to literally drop off. Eyebrows and eyelashes disappear. The disease often attacks the larynx, giving the voice a rasping, grating sound. The odor of a leper is unmistakable and is not pleasant.

Believe it or not, in the ancient world the social and religious consequences of leprosy were as painful as the physical disfigurement itself. The Jews abhorred leprosy. More than any other disease, it was interpreted as a curse imposed by divine wrath. There were over sixty different causes for defilement in the

Mosaic Law. Touching a leper was second only to the defilement incurred by contact with a dead body.

The Law was clear and firm: "The person with such an infectious disease must wear torn clothes, let his hair be unkempt, cover the lower part of his face and cry out, 'Unclean! Unclean!' As long as he has the infection he remains unclean. He must live alone; he must live outside the camp" (Leviticus 13:45-46).

Leprosy was a living death, an inescapable prison! During Jesus' day lepers were permitted to attend synagogue, but were isolated and quarantined in a booth set off to the side. In the Middle Ages the priest would lead the leper into church and there read the burial service over him. It was their way of saying that, for all practical purposes, he was dead.

There never has been a disease that so radically separated a man from his fellow-man. It was the AIDS of the ancient world.

Why? Because the effect of leprosy on the body symbolized the effect of sin on the soul! This does not mean that lepers were themselves personally more sinful than others. It was the disease, not its victim, that portrayed the disfiguring impact of sin. This is why whenever Jesus ministered to lepers He is said to "cleanse" them of their disease rather than "heal" them (cf. Matthew 8:3, 10:8). In other words, leprosy symbolized spiritual defilement.

All this makes it quite remarkable that a leper should approach Jesus in the presence of a large crowd. This man had to have known that the Law required him to stand aloof and apart from non-lepers. He had to have known he risked being stoned should he draw near. As he came to Jesus he no doubt shouted, in humiliation, "Unclean! Unclean!" Alerted to his approach, the crowd would have scattered in every direction.

Why was he so bold? Perhaps he saw something in Jesus that he had never seen in any other human being. Perhaps he sensed a tender mercy and compassion that no one else possessed. Somehow he knew that Jesus was neither afraid of him nor repulsed by his disease.

Our Lord's response is astounding! He "reached out his hand, and touched the man." Any other man would not have come within six feet of the leper, as required by law. Some even insisted that if you were standing down-wind from a leper you had to remain at least 150 feet away! What we must understand is that no one, absolutely and literally *no one*, ever touched a leper on purpose. No one, that is, except Jesus!

Jesus certainly could have cleansed this leper without getting so close. He could have merely spoken the word or instructed him to wash in the river Jordan (as did Elisha in 2 Kings 5:10-14), or by some other method (cf. Matthew 8:5-13). Why did Jesus touch him? Mark tells us what Matthew probably assumed we would take for granted. Jesus touched the leper because He was "filled with compassion" (Mark 1:41). Jesus dared to touch what everyone else found repulsive. Such was the depth of His mercy.

Have you ever noticed how Christians act upon entering a church meeting? They shake hands, pat one another on the back, even hug and kiss. There is a reason for that. We all want tangible, touchable signs of affection and acceptance. At home my two daughters would rather wrestle with me and play "tickle time" than anything else. There's something about the physical embrace that is unique and unparalleled in communicating love.

No one in the ancient world was more desperate for physical contact than the leper. He yearned for a touch, any touch. Ever since he contracted the disease he had been cut off from physical interaction with others. Luke tells us this leper was "covered with leprosy" (Luke 5:12), indicating that the disease was in an advanced stage. In other words, this man had been suffering for years . . . years without ever knowing the joy of someone's tender touch . . . years of complete physical isolation.

How can words express what this man felt when the hand of Jesus made contact with his disfigured flesh! He looked about and saw everyone standing back, everyone holding their noses, everyone hiding their eyes, everyone except Jesus. Jesus walked over . . . and touched him!

When the Lord brings us into contact with the social lepers of our day, love demands a touch. We can't just love them from a distance. When the outcasts and the offensive and the bothersome move toward us in their misery, when everyone else turns away, holding their noses, love demands that we extend the hand of Jesus and touch them . . . both physically and personally.

This remarkable story about the leper is found in Matthew 8.

So what? Simply this. Matthew 5–7 is the record of Jesus' Sermon on the Mount. He preached the most famous sermon ever heard . . . and then came back down to touch a leper! If you're like me, you'd just as soon stay on the mountain top. It's a lot safer sitting as Jesus lectures, taking notes, arguing about what this or that declaration might mean. That's fine, so long as when the sermon is over we too come back down and extend the tender touch of mercy to the "lepers" in our society, perhaps even in our own church.

To what lengths, love? Jesus just showed us. How deep, how radical, how far must mercy go? Jesus just showed us. No custom, no manmade law, no natural revulsion we might feel in the pit of our stomach, can stand in the way of Christian love. So the next time you're tempted to pull away, remember what Jesus said: "As I have loved you, so you must love one another" (John 13:34).

NINE

Where Never Is Heard a Discouraging Word

There was once a powerful king who, out of curiosity, commissioned one of his servants to bring him the most valuable and powerful commodity in the realm. Upon his return the servant approached the king with a silver platter, and on it a human tongue. Fascinated, the king again sent him out, this time to find the most dangerous and destructive commodity in the realm. Once more, he returned with the same silver platter, and on it another human tongue. Well and wisely did Solomon say, "The tongue has the power of life and death, and those who love it will eat its fruit" (Proverbs 18:21).

THE POWER OF THE TONGUE

Many volumes have been written since World War II in an attempt to understand Adolph Hitler's rise to power. There are political explanations and economic explanations and military explanations and even religious explanations of how he was able to apply such a remarkable stranglehold on the German people. William Shirer, author of *The Rise and Fall of the Third Reich*, attributes much of Hitler's success to his oratorical skill. He possessed an uncanny knack for mesmerizing his audiences with a magical (and some say demonic) power of speech.

Hitler himself once said that one of the more significant events of his life occurred in a lecture hall in 1918. There he rashly intervened to refute a man who had spoken approvingly of the Jewish people. "All at once," Hitler later would write, "I was offered an opportunity of speaking before a large audience; and the thing that I had always presumed from pure feeling without knowing it was now corroborated: I could speak!"[1] I need not remind you of the powerful impact of Hitler's speaking ability on an entire nation. Solomon was right. The tongue does indeed have the power of life and death.

The tongue can manipulate public opinion and shape social policy. Have you noticed how behavior once considered immoral has been sanitized through a subtle shift in terminology? For example, people don't commit adultery anymore. They have "affairs." Teenagers aren't promiscuous, nor do they engage in fornication. Rather, they are "sexually active." We rarely hear about drug addiction or "dope." The preferred vocabulary is "chemical dependency" or "substance abuse." Men aren't sodomites. They simply are pursuing an "alternative lifestyle." Women don't kill their unborn babies. Instead, they "terminate pregnancies." It is frightening how attitudes toward morality are being unconsciously shaped by a simple shift in terminology. Such is the power of words.

The tongue has the power of either easing or adding to the burdens people bear. One well-timed word of encouragement can change someone's life for the good. I think we would be surprised if we knew the number of people who would never have achieved their life's goal were it not for a word of encouragement or appreciation from a caring friend. This is what Solomon had in mind when he said that, "An anxious heart weighs a man down, but a kind word cheers him up" (Proverbs 12:25). Or again, "Pleasant words are a honeycomb, sweet to the soul and healing to the bones" (16:24).

But it is also frightening to think that some people carry indelible emotional scars because of a simple careless comment. "Reckless words pierce like a sword" (12:18), and many have felt their razor sharp edge. Yes, words can heal, but they can also inflict indescribably painful wounds. We must never forget that, "the tongue that brings healing is a tree of life, but a deceitful tongue crushes the spirit" (15:4).

THE POWER OF ENCOURAGEMENT

The Apostle Paul must have been a student of the Proverbs, for his letters are filled with praise, appreciation, and compliments. He must have known, as did Solomon, that burdens are eased and spirits elevated and relationships healed by words of encouragement. I noticed this in one passage in particular, again in the book of Philippians.

The congregation at Philippi was probably as close to an ideal church as you will find in either Scripture or subsequent history, but that does not mean it was free of all problems. A dispute between two women threatened the peace of the church and was evidently serious enough to call for immediate action on Paul's part. People were perhaps beginning to take sides in the squabble, and the leaders had either been ineffective in their efforts to end it or possibly even indifferent to the whole mess.

But Paul is determined to put a stop to it before things get too far out of hand. There's really nothing surprising about that. What is especially instructive, though, is the way he goes about doing it. Read carefully what he says:

> Therefore, my brothers, you whom I love and long for, my joy and crown, that is how you should stand firm in the Lord, dear friends! I plead with Euodia and I plead with Syntyche to agree with each other in the Lord. Yes, and I ask you, loyal yokefellow, help these women who have contended at my side in the cause of the gospel, along with Clement and the rest of my fellow workers, whose names are in the book of life. (Philippians 4:1-3)

As to the cause of this dispute, your guess is as good as mine. After more than fifteen years in pastoral ministry I've come to the conclusion that anything's possible. A friend once observed that, sin being what it is, Christians are capable of just about everything except blasphemy of the Holy Spirit!

I came across an illustration of this soon after my father died. It's customary at a time like that to search back through one's family history. Nostalgia can be a soothing balm to the grief-stricken. My aunt found a copy of the history of Providence Church, the small congregation north of Liberty, Missouri, where my grandfather and grandmother had been married. A few of the incidents recorded in that volume confirm my belief that, sadly, Christians can become involved in virtually every kind of squabble.

For example, one member (I've omitted all names to protect the innocent!) was excommunicated for disrupting a church service. He had jumped to his feet yelling after being hit in the back of the head by a man's hat that had been tossed, frisbee style, across the auditorium during a sermon. I can't imagine disciplining someone for such a minor offence. (But then there's no record of *what* he yelled!).

Another gentleman who had been rejected by a young lady decided to seek vengeance on the rival who had won her affection. During a Sunday morning service he quietly slipped out the back door, located the team of horses belonging to this man, pulled out a knife and proceeded to cut off their tails.

Then there's the fellow described as being,

> a good six feet tall and over two-hundred pounds, tap-dancer par excellence, light on his feet and cat-quick; he could move across the dance floor as quiet as baby shoes on the bare boards. His natural ability could have commanded top-billing with salary to match in any theater. Although David danced before the Lord in the Holy Scriptures, for [him] it was considered a sin, and he was excommunicated.

Finally, the document tells the story of an irate parishioner who piled wood shavings in the middle of the church sanctuary and set them ablaze. Thus the original structure of Providence Church burned to the ground in 1880!

Forgive me this brief excursion into my family's past, but it illustrates well that Christians are capable of some bizarre forms of behavior. Euodia and Syntyche were no exception, but I trust they never resorted to the extreme measures employed by certain members of that little church in Missouri.

What is of special interest to us, however, is the way Paul

dealt with the problem. The leaders of Providence Church were evidently quick to excommunicate an errant member. Paul took another approach. Yes, he does plead and urge that these ladies come to peaceful terms with each other. But note carefully what Paul says before that. Paul begins in verse 1 by addressing these Christians in Philippi as "brothers," men and women whom he "loves and longs for." These people, including Euodia and Syntyche, are his "joy and crown." They are "dear friends," literally, "beloved ones."

Is there any special reason why Paul should begin chapter 4 of his letter in this way? Should we dismiss these terms of affection and appreciation as little more than literary formalities? I don't think so. This is more than a casual salutation. Paul prefaced his *commanding* with *commending*.

Be it noted that what Paul said of the Philippians was true. He wasn't the sort to fabricate praise of the unworthy. He really meant what he said. After all, even Euodia and Syntyche had proven themselves as able coworkers at his side (verse 3). They had given sacrificially of themselves in the cause of the gospel, and Paul is not one to ignore their service. But why does he mention all that at this point in his letter?

Paul knew that *exhortation is always more effective when preceded by encouragement.* People are always more open to justified rebuke if they first know that you care for them as individuals and are appreciative of their efforts. Euodia and Syntyche were wrong in how they had behaved. The other Philippian believers were wrong in permitting this dispute to get out of hand. But there were several things about them that were right, and Paul takes advantage of the opportunity to mention those positive things.

He begins by addressing them as "brothers." They are together members of a spiritual family, united not by their own blood but by that of Jesus. This isn't the case of an outsider poking his nose into matters that don't concern him. This is a family affair. Perhaps it is also Paul's subtle way of reminding Euodia and Syntyche that they are *sisters* in this family.

The second thing Paul does is reaffirm his love for the Philippian Christians. "You whom I love" is literally "beloved," the same word he uses at the close of verse 1, where it is translated as "dear friends." My hunch is that Euodia and Syntyche and the other believers in Philippi were quick to heed Paul's plea. My hunch is that any resentment on their part soon gave way to repentance. I base my hunch on the fact that they knew from the outset that Paul loved them. He isn't like a king lording it over his subjects. It isn't ecclesiastical authority but personal affection that prompts his rebuke, and you can be sure that they knew it. The lesson is clear: If you don't really care about someone, don't confront him.

Meaningful involvement in someone's life must precede any effort to expose his sin. Your ability to receive my criticism is largely determined by how persuaded you are that I really care. A lot of people in the local church are little more than self-appointed ministers of confrontation, for the simple reason that they enjoy it. When the thrill of power is mixed with the satisfaction of self-righteousness, the results can be devastating.[2]

Paul, on the other hand, not only loves these believers, he longs to be with them. The pain of geographical separation is almost more than he can bear. He recalls with fond affection the time he spent in Philippi, ministering to them and they to him.

You are my joy! You are my crown! Charlie Brown may find happiness in a warm puppy, but Paul would look no further than these fellow believers. In fact, says Paul, whatever reward the Lord may have in store for me, it is inseparable from you Philippians and your progress in the faith.

Be honest with yourself. If you were Euodia or Syntyche, would you be inclined to accept Paul's judgment and respond to his plea? I certainly would, knowing from his words of encouragement that he is confronting my sin only because he deeply cares for my soul.

That is what differentiates encouragement from mere flattery. "Whoever flatters his neighbor is spreading a net for his feet" (Proverbs 29:5, cf. Romans 16:18). The flatterer is motivated by what your response will do for *him*. Encouragement always has the best interests of the other person in view. The flatterer uses words of praise and appreciation to disarm you and to put you at ease. Then, when you are relaxed in his presence and have entrusted yourself to his care, he springs his trap.

When Paul spoke highly of the Philippians, he had no ulterior motive. Larry Crabb has described encouragement as the careful selection of words "that are intended to influence another person meaningfully toward increased godliness."[3] That is precisely what Paul is doing. The goal of his encouragement is godliness.

THE LIMITS OF ENCOURAGEMENT

But encouragement can't do everything. When you seek to encourage a Christian friend who is feeling unloved and unimportant, nothing you say or do can make them any more secure or significant than they already are. Only Christ Jesus can provide for those fundamental needs. Only He can fill that God-shaped vacuum. We must never envision our encouragement as something we do to supplement or make up for something God has failed to do. The love God has for His children can neither be enhanced nor diminished by the action of any person, friend or foe.

My most diligent efforts to encourage you will not in any way induce God to love you more than He already does. And if I should fail to express my appreciation for your gifts and ministry it will in no way make you any less valuable or precious to the heart of your heavenly Father.

What encouragement can and should do is put you in touch with the reality of God's love and purpose for your life. I am but an earthly instrument of Christ Jesus, and the goal of my encouragement is to sensitize your heart to the unconditional affection He has for you. Words of appreciation and gestures of love and acceptance enhance not the fact but the *feeling* of security and significance. "The situation," says Crabb, "is much like a man who discovers that there is oil beneath my property. He does not make me wealthy; I was rich before he found the oil, but it is not until he makes me aware of the oil that I experience my wealth."[4]

Clearly, then, we are not talking about a technique or method, or even a specially selected and carefully articulated group of words. To think in those terms is to engage in manipulation, not ministry. Encouragement is fundamentally an attitude, or better still a commitment. It is a willingness to risk rejection and ridicule in order to touch someone who is hurting and who cannot be trusted to respond appreciatively to your efforts.

THE ENEMY OF ENCOURAGEMENT

Our reluctance to encourage others would seem to be related to something I spoke of earlier, namely, our commitment to self-protection. It is virtually impossible to help someone else without running the risk of being hurt in the process. There is a strange irony at work here. On the one hand, we have a brother or sister who feels utterly worthless, aching on the inside to be accepted in spite of their obvious shortcomings. But, on the other hand, it is our need for precisely the same thing that inhibits us from reaching out to them. We fear that in opening up our own soul to meet their need for love, *our own need* will go unnoticed.

What we fail to grasp, says Crabb, is that, "God's acceptance [of us in Christ] makes anyone else's rejection no more devastating than a misplaced dollar would be to a millionaire. We foolishly believe that other people's acceptance represents a legitimate measure of our value."[5] And we will continue foolishly to believe it until we come to firm grips with the truth we discovered in chapter 7. Until you realize that Jesus is enough, you will persist in selfishly seeking from others what only He can provide.

TWO OBJECTIONS

Not all of you will agree with what I have said about the role encouragement plays in bearing one another's burdens. I know this is the case because of a comment someone once made to me in the course of a conversation on this very topic. Concerning encouragement, he said: "Some can't give it and some don't need it." I couldn't disagree more.

Encouragement is something *everyone can do*. And encouragement is something *everyone must have*. Every Christian is called upon to encourage others. And contrary to what you may be thinking, *you* are not an exception. The author of the Epistle to the Hebrews is addressing the entire Christian community when he says, "Encourage one another daily, as long as it is called Today, so that none of you may be hardened by sin's deceitfulness" (Hebrews 3:13).

Why do you go to church? No, it's not a silly question. Why do you go to church? What is your reason for showing up on Sunday morning and perhaps again at night or on Wednesday? Fill in the blank: "I'm going to church next Sunday in order that I may ________." What did you say? "Hear the Word of God?" "Praise and worship the Lord Jesus Christ?" "Teach a Sunday school class?" There's nothing wrong with any of those answers. But listen again to the author of Hebrews: "Let us not give up meeting together, as some are in the habit of doing, but *let us encourage one another*—and all the more as you see the Day approaching" (Hebrews 10:25, emphasis added). Notice the contrast: "Let us not give up meeting," versus, "Let us encourage one another." In other words, to Paul, "going to church" and "encouraging one another" were practically synonymous.

Can you even remotely envision what your church would be like if only a handful of its members came each Sunday with the goal of encouraging others with words and gestures and acts of appreciation and praise and love and acceptance? Dare we even dream of it? Encouragement is something *everyone* can (and should) do.

Encouragement is also something everyone must *receive*. I'm not prone to depression or despondency. But there are times when I need to know that someone cares, and that I'm not just spinning my pastoral wheels. These past few years have been especially difficult for our church, due to the slumping economy and the dip in oil prices. Several families who were actively involved in positions of leadership and ministry have been forced to move away in search of employment. It's enough to discourage even the most optimistic of pastors.

Evidently I'm not the only one aware of this. Just this past week I received a call from one of the men on our board of elders. He didn't have a lot to say, other than to encourage and reassure me how deeply he and his family appreciated my ministry. The conversation couldn't have lasted for more than a minute or two, but as Solomon once wrote, "Like apples of gold in settings of silver is a word spoken in [the] right circumstances" (Proverbs

25:11, NASB). This man's goal was not to stroke my ego, but to remind me that, the most adverse of situations notwithstanding, God had placed me here to minister to his family and to others. His brief word of encouragement quickly reminded me that my value is not measured by the number of people to whom I preach, but by the approval of our heavenly Father.

It's reassuring to know that even that great encourager, the Apostle Paul, needed encouragement. During his final imprisonment, shortly preceding his execution, he wrote these urgent words to young Timothy: "Do your best to come to me quickly, for Demas, because he loved this world, has deserted me and has gone to Thessalonica. Crescens has gone to Galatia, and Titus to Dalmatia. Only Luke is with me. Get Mark and bring him with you, because he is helpful to me in my ministry" (2 Timothy 4:9-11).

This man who had boldly defied the enemies of the gospel and suffered innumerable hardships is desperate for the encouragement of a close friend. He longs for the comfort and sustenance that only another Christian can give. Paul longs for the coming of Christ Jesus (verse 8), but until that day should arrive he also longs for the coming of Timothy (verse 9)!

We are not left wondering why he felt the need for Timothy's actual, physical presence: "Demas has abandoned me! He loved this world better than he loved Christ or the gospel or me. I'm all alone, except for Luke. I need you and Mark right now. Please come quickly."

Interwoven into this simple plea are two truths concerning encouragement that we must observe. First, did you catch those names: Demas . . . Mark? Do they ring a bell in your biblical memory? Demas had formerly been one of Paul's dearest and closest friends, one of his most trustworthy and hardworking companions (cf. Colossians 4:14, Philemon 24). His defection must have been especially distressing to Paul. Evidently Demas was faithful, vocal, and diligent as long as it was easy, as long as not too many demands were made, as long as it was convenient to be a Christian. But in Paul's most critical hour of need, Demas had deserted him.

But not all news is bad. "Get Mark and bring him with you, because he is helpful to me in my ministry." Mark? Could this be the same Mark who, on his own initiative, had abandoned Paul during the second missionary journey (Acts 12:25, 13:13, 15:36-41)? In one sense, yes, it is the same Mark. But in another sense, he is an altogether different man. How had Mark been restored to such a place of prominence and personal importance in Paul's ministry? What can account for his remarkable turnabout? Nowhere in the New Testament are we told, but I would like to make a suggestion.

I don't believe it is coincidental that Mark remained with Barnabas following the break-up with Paul. Barnabas, whose name means "son of encouragement," must have had a hand in Mark's recovery. Peter, too, was an influence on his life (1 Peter 5:13). I can't prove it, but my hunch is that, when it came to Mark, Barnabas was true to his name. My hunch is that Peter, who himself knew a little about failure and restoration, was also quick to encourage this young man, even as the Lord Jesus had encouraged *him* (cf. John 21). Just think of it. This man who had once let Paul down is now summoned along with Timothy as a dependable source of encouragement!

The second thing I want you to note is found a bit further on in 2 Timothy 4. In verses 16-17 Paul writes: "At my first defense, no one came to my support, but everyone deserted me. May it not be held against them. But the Lord stood at my side and gave me strength, so that through me the message might be fully proclaimed and all the Gentiles might hear it. And I was delivered from the lion's mouth."

Let me come right to the point. Paul knew at the time of his trial and at the time he wrote these words to Timothy that the Lord was at his side, strengthening him. Paul knew that should Timothy and Luke and Crescens and Titus and Mark all abandon him, even as Demas had, Christ Jesus would never leave him nor forsake him. And yet he still feels the need for the encouraging presence of these friends.

It isn't because he has lingering doubts about the sufficiency of the Lord. Paul still believed that Jesus was enough. But he wants Timothy and Luke and Mark and others at his side because they are the principal way in which Christ encourages him. It is not a question of either Christ *or* Christian friends. It is Christ *through* Christian friends. Their encouraging presence is the medium through which the Lord Jesus strengthens and sustains Paul in his final and most severe test.

Yes, encouragement is something everyone, even Mark, can do. And yes, encouragement is something everyone, even Paul, must have. So what are we waiting for?

TEN

Meekness, Rebounds, and Licorice Seeds!

It's a good thing physical examinations are not required for entrance into the Christian ministry. If they were, odds are I'd flunk. Of course, even to suggest that a person must meet specified physical criteria before serving God in an official capacity probably strikes all of us as outlandish.

But what may seem ludicrous to us was divine law during Old Testament times. It wasn't enough that a young man be of the tribe of Levi and the family of Aaron. It wasn't enough that he aspire to serve as high priest before God. If he had a tattoo on his body he was disqualified! If he had a bald spot on his head he was disqualified! If he was lame or had a deformed limb or a broken foot or hand, he was disqualified. If he suffered from eczema or any other serious skin condition he was barred from serving. And if all that were not enough, neither the hunchback nor the dwarf nor the man who had married a widow or divorced woman was qualified to be the high priest.

This all sounds foreign to us, and we are relieved that the New Testament imposes no such physical standards. But that doesn't mean there are no qualifications for ministry—that just anyone can do anything in the local church.

Certainly we're all aware of the qualifications required of leaders in the Church: "If anyone sets his heart on being an overseer [elder]," says Paul, "he desires a noble task. Now the overseer must be above reproach, the husband of but one wife, temperate, self-controlled, respectable, hospitable," and he goes on to list other qualifications that testify to the potential elder's maturity (1 Timothy 3:1-2). Deacons likewise must fulfill certain spiritual and moral requirements (verses 8-13).

But what about the kind of ministry that has concerned us in this book? Are there any special qualifications necessary to bear one another's burdens? What does it take to become meaningfully and mercifully involved in the life of someone who is hurting? Are there any spiritual characteristics that are indispensable for the task we've been discussing?

We know that gender, age, height, race, and other such physical considerations are irrelevant when it comes to serving one another in the Body of Christ. That responsibility falls on each and every believer. Of that we may be sure. But I do believe there are a few character traits that are essential for effective ministry. In this chapter I want to focus on the most critical one of all.

MEEKNESS AND MERCY

It strikes me as more than coincidental that in the verse immediately preceding Paul's command that we bear one another's burdens (Galatians 6:2), he talks about a "spirit of gentleness" (6:1, NASB). The word he uses is *prautes*, often translated "meekness." Only three verses prior to that, in Galatians 5:23, *prautes* is listed as one of the fruits of the Holy Spirit. And when Jesus said, "Blessed are the meek, for they will inherit the earth" (Matthew 5:5), the word He employed was *praus* (also translated "gentle" or "humble").

If you are wondering why I've selected this particular virtue from among all the others mentioned in the New Testament, I can only say it comes from years of observing how Christians relate to each other in a local church setting. *There is simply no denying that the most successful Christian servants are those who have learned to deal gently and humbly with others* (cf. 2 Timothy 2:24-25). Meekness is indispensable to a ministry of mercy. Without it there is little hope that anyone will profit from your efforts.

I want us to think about this in some depth. I want us to understand not only what it means to be meek, but also what its moral antithesis is and how it must be overcome. So remember, it's okay if you have eczema or a bald spot on your head or a broken hand. You can still bear someone's burdens and help bring them to maturity in Christ. But without humility of spirit, without meekness and gentleness of heart, you don't stand much of a chance.

IS MEEKNESS WEAKNESS?

I think it was Bobby Knight, boisterous coach of the Indiana Hoosiers college basketball team, who said, "The meek may well inherit the earth, but they rarely get rebounds!" It's too bad Mr. Knight is not as competent in theology as he is in coaching basketball. He is simply echoing a distorted notion of meekness or humility shared by most people today.

When Jesus pronounced a blessing on the "meek" or "humble,"[1] He did not intend to preclude Christians from playing hard-nosed basketball! Contrary to what you may think, one can be physically powerful, athletically aggressive, *and* humble, all at the same time. It isn't the indolent, weak, cowardly, or mentally flabby person that Jesus blessed. Nor is that the kind of individual who is best equipped to lovingly bear the burdens of others. Our image of the humble person as some timid soul who walks with slumped shoulders and only rarely voices his opinion needs serious revision.

So what does it mean to be meek? What is humility?

Let me first make clear one important point. In our desire to differentiate meekness from weakness, we must not lose sight of one vital element in this virtue: *Sensitivity.* In our zeal to prove Bobby Knight wrong, we must acknowledge that involved in meekness is a capacity to deal gently with others. When the gospel is at stake, or when sin poses a threat, the meek can and must be tough. But when people are hurting, the meek must be tender. The calloused and uncaring leave only scars on the Body of Christ.

The meek person is the one whose touch is not only sensitive but also tactful. His words are filled with compassion; he always responds with tenderness, even to those who are maliciously abusive. And he does all this without in any way compromising the truth!

I think you know the kind of individual I have in mind. He always seems to know when to speak and what to say, and never sounds artificial when he does it. People respond to him, because he motivates them not by intimidation or rebuke but by encouragement. He is remarkably discerning, always aware when a brother or sister is experiencing deep emotional pain. Would that we all could display such a biblical blend of conviction and compassion!

I'm fascinated by the way this delicate balance was maintained by Jesus. No sooner had He clenched His fist to drive the money changers from the temple than He extended an open hand to heal those who were blind and lame (Matthew 21:12-14)! Joni Eareckson Tada reminds us,

> There is no room in Scripture for a one-sided view of our Lord. He points an angry, righteous finger at the hypocrites on one hand, yet reaches down to gently touch the need of the lowly with the other. He turns a face as hard as steel to the religious phonies yet smiles encouragement at those who reach to Him in simple faith.[2]

All this, mind you, from one "gentle and humble in heart" (Matthew 11:29).

THE MARROW OF MEEKNESS

But I still haven't touched on the heart of humility. One particular element in this virtue does more than anything else to heal relationships and soothe the soul's distress. A word of warning, though: This aspect of humility isn't especially easy. (But then you didn't expect it to be, did you?) It isn't something we come by naturally. It is found only in the overflow of divine grace. Martyn Lloyd-Jones hinted at it in his comments on Matthew 5:5:

> I can see my own utter nothingness and helplessness face to face with the demands of the gospel and the Law of God. I am aware, when I am honest with myself, of the sin and the

> evil that are within me, and that drag me down. And I am ready to face both these things. But how much more difficult it is to allow other people to say things like that about me! I instinctively resent it. We all of us prefer to condemn ourselves than to allow somebody else to condemn us.[3]

Did you pick up on what he is saying? What is the heart of humility? What is the marrow of meekness? It is *the willingness to allow others to say about me the same things I readily acknowledge before God.* That's tough to do! When I'm on my knees, alone in the presence of the infinitely Holy God, confessing my sinfulness is not so hard. There is no place to hide, no secret that I can possibly conceal. But I instinctively recoil and become indignant and defensive when *someone else* dares to suggest that I am what I just told God I am! That's an embarrassing and painful admission, but it has to be made.

If you and I aren't willing to let others say about us what we know is true, our efforts to help them will be fruitless. I'm not suggesting that it is good for them to speak to you in those terms (although at times it is essential that they do so). It is often downright discourteous and cruel, depending on the circumstances. But that person must see for himself that you are willing to be humiliated for his sake before your ministry will be received.

To the degree that you insist on protecting your own reputation, you will fail to leave a lasting and meaningful impact on another person. Jesus succeeded because, though He was God, He "made himself nothing, taking the very nature of a servant, being made in human likeness. And being found in appearance as a man, he humbled himself and became obedient to death—even death on a cross!" (Philippians 2:7-8).

Are you and I willing to be humbled in the eyes and ears of others? Or shall we insist on clinging to our reputation, regardless of what the cost may be to someone else? It's a truism, but I'll say it anyway. *Self-protection and self-sacrifice are mutually exclusive.* They cannot coexist. We must opt for one or the other. I cannot give myself to you as long as I insist on protecting myself from the emotional pain you may choose to inflict. If I'm not willing to accept the latter, I'll never succeed in the former.

THE ENEMY

But knowing what humility or meekness is constitutes only half the story. We must also be wary of its moral and spiritual antithesis. It isn't so much pride that I have in mind, but one of its particularly destructive effects.

Have you ever wondered why films starring Clint Eastwood, Sylvester Stallone, or Charles Bronson do so phenomenally well at the box-office? If you've seen any of their more recent movies you know it isn't because of their thespian skills! These men appeal to the public because they enable us to experience vicariously the sweet taste of *revenge*.

Each of us secretly enjoys the thrill of "getting even" with someone who has wronged us. Since the law frowns on such behavior, we pay our $5 at the ticket window to watch others do it for us. We draw a bizarre sense of satisfaction in watching a muscle-bound Hollywood hero get even with the kind of people we dislike.

The other day I saw a bumper-sticker that suggested: AVENGE YOURSELF: LIVE LONG ENOUGH TO BE A PROBLEM TO YOUR CHILDREN! I know . . . I laughed too. But remember that meekness is the moral antithesis of the spirit of revenge. Nothing is more contrary to the spirit of humility than that deep-seated urge to settle a score.

I've made several confessions about myself. It is now public knowledge that I'm both a mechanical idiot and an incurable romantic. Bear with me one more time. I am (literally) a card-carrying member of The Andy Griffith Show Appreciation Society. There's something very appealing about the simple pleasures of life in Mayberry, North Carolina.

In one episode, Andy and his young son, Opie, engage in a conversation that goes something like this:

Andy: "Where are you going son?"
Opie: "Over to Jerry Parker's. Me and him are making a trade: His roller-skates for my licorice seeds."
Andy: "Licorice seeds? What are licorice seeds? And where did you get them?"

Opie: "On another trade with Tommy Farrell. I gave him my cap-pistol."
Andy: "Your new one?"
Opie: "Yeah. And it would have been worth it to grow my own licorice sticks. But it was a fake. I planted them, but nothing came up. Pa, I think Tommy cheated me."
Andy: "Yes, son, I'd say so. So now you're gonna' pawn 'em off on the next fella'?"
Opie: "And on a better trade too! Roller-skates are a lot better than a cap-pistol."
Andy: "You know you've been taught the Golden Rule, 'Do unto others as you would have them do unto you.' Do you think you've been living by it?"
Opie: "Sure, Pa. Tommy did it unto me and now I'm gonna' do it unto Jerry!"

Trust me. Andy straightened out Opie on his misinterpretation of the Golden Rule.

The fact is, each of us has an innate urge to do it unto someone else once it has been done to us. It doesn't matter who is on the receiving end, just as long as we get in our licks. But the Apostle Paul couldn't have said it more clearly:

> Do not repay anyone evil for evil. . . . Do not take revenge, my friends, but leave room for God's wrath, for it is written: "It is mine to avenge; I will repay," says the Lord. On the contrary: "If your enemy is hungry, feed him; if he is thirsty, give him something to drink. In doing this, you will heap burning coals on his head." Do not be overcome by evil, but overcome evil with good. (Romans 12:17,19-21)

Invariably someone will object to this, pointing to the Old Testament *lex talionis*, the law of retaliation. "How can Paul say that," comes the cry of protest, "when the Old Testament endorses 'an eye for an eye and a tooth for a tooth' (Exodus 21:22-25, Leviticus 24:18-20)? And wasn't it Moses, reportedly the meekest man on the earth (Numbers 12:3), who wrote it?" That's a pretty good question.

First, we must remember that the point of this Old Testament law was to ensure that punishment was proportionate to the offense. The penalty must fit the crime. The phrase "eye for an eye" was itself simply a formula. Rarely if ever was it literally applied. It only meant that compensation had to be appropriate to the loss incurred.

The man who killed an ox, for example, didn't necessarily have to replace it with another ox. He could pay its owner enough for him to buy another. Only in the case of premeditated murder was compensation forbidden. In the case of murder, "a life for a life" was literally demanded (Numbers 35:16-34).

The second thing to remember is that the *lex talionis* was not only fair and just, it was also extremely effective. It was immensely successful in preventing blood-feuds and tribal warfare. Do you recall this conversation between Huckleberry Finn and Buck?

> "What's a feud, Buck?"
>
> "Why, where was you raised, Huck? Don't you know what a feud is?"
>
> "Never heard of it before—tell me about it."
>
> "Well," says Buck, "a feud is this way: A man has a quarrel with another man, and kills him; then that other man's brother kills him; then the other brothers, on both sides, goes for one another; then the cousins chip in—and by and by everybody's killed off, and there ain't no more feud. But it's kind of slow and takes a long time."[4]

That is precisely what the *lex talionis* was designed to prevent! If the initial offense is met with a fair and proportionate penalty, that's the end of the matter.

Finally, this particular law fell within the domain of public, civil justice. It was not a law endorsing personal revenge. The intent of the law of retaliation was to undermine the personal vendetta. It was an instrument of the court, a means of satisfying the legal demands and penal sanctions of the state. We must be careful that we do not transfer to our private affairs a law which carried force only in the public domain.

Paul's counsel, therefore, is perfectly compatible with the Old Testament. But note well that he doesn't stop with forbidding revenge. Clearly, forbearance is only one-half of our responsibility. It isn't enough merely to refrain from retaliation. It isn't enough to control the impulse to "get even." Anyone can suppress the urge to strike back, even the nonChristian. The Christian, says Paul, must go a step beyond. The Christian not only must not retaliate, he must also seek *to do good* to those who mistreat him. "If your enemy is hungry," says Paul, "feed him; if he is thirsty, give him something to drink. In doing this, you will heap burning coals on his head" (Romans 12:20).

What does he mean when he says that by doing good to those who do us harm we "will heap burning coals on his head"? Are the burning coals a symbol of the irritation and aggravation our enemy will experience when he sees us respond to his evil with good? We might like to think so. But it seems unlikely, for isn't that just a round-about way of getting even after all?

Perhaps Paul is describing the burning sense of shame and remorse our enemy feels when he sees how his evil has been met with kindness. Or the burning coals might be a metaphor for the melting down of his anger by the power of our mercy. There was an ancient Egyptian ritual in which a man would give public evidence of his repentance by carrying a pan of burning charcoal on his head. Might this be the imagery behind Paul's words? Whatever the case, Paul's point seems to be that the best (though admittedly not the most pleasant) way to handle an enemy is to transform him into a friend.

Not everyone, however, will take this advice sitting down. After all, it's one thing for Paul to tell us not to punch an enemy, but it's something else to suggest that we should pray for him! But that is what the apostle says, and there can be no doubt that he is echoing the ethic of Jesus.

When our Lord addressed Himself to the problem of anger, He let it be known that suppressing your enmity is a bare minimum. It isn't enough just to control the outward display of our feelings, all the while permitting the spirit of alienation to fester secretly and out of sight. Here is what He said:

> You have heard that it was said to the people long ago, "Do not murder, and anyone who murders will be subject to

> judgment." But I tell you that anyone who is angry with his brother will be subject to judgment. Again, anyone who says to his brother, "Raca," is answerable to the Sanhedrin. But anyone who says, "You fool!" will be in danger of the fire of hell. Therefore, if you are offering your gift at the altar and there remember that your brother has something against you, leave your gift there in front of the altar. First go and be reconciled to your brother; then come and offer your gift. (Matthew 5:21-24)

His point is that we have to deal with the inner resentment and bitterness that lead to outbursts of hostility. Otherwise we are merely substituting one form of Pharisaism for another.

What this tells me is that the meek are always quick to make up. They are "peacemakers" (Matthew 5:9) at heart. Don't you find it interesting that Jesus doesn't single out the guilty party and insist that he take the initiative? *Both* parties are responsible to make the first move, regardless of who is to blame.

Furthermore, there is no indication in what Jesus says that the grievance your brother has against you must be *justifiable* before action is required on your part. In other words, even if someone else simply thinks that he has a right to be angry with you, take steps to put out the fire. He may have no legitimate grounds for his complaint—but Jesus evidently didn't think that was relevant.

This may all sound good in theory, but what if the other person adamantly refuses your efforts at reconciliation? Even meekness can't always work miracles. The answer to this is found in something else Paul said in Romans 12: "If it is possible, as far as it depends on you, live at peace with everyone" (verse 18).

Here we see both the idealism and the realism of Holy Scripture. Ideally, we should live peaceably with others. But Paul knew all too well, as do you and I, that peace isn't always possible.

But be careful. When he says "if it is possible," he is not referring to some inability arising from *your* weakness. We cannot give up on the pursuit of peace simply because we ourselves are quick-tempered, unable to restrain our impulses, or simply too bitter to control our resentment toward the other person.

Paul's words are not a loophole for us to avoid reconciliation.

The "if it is possible" has to do entirely with the other person's response to our initiative. I've known a few people, as I'm sure you have, whose spirit and temperament made reconciliation impossible (at least from a human point of view). We are not masters over the feelings and beliefs of others. There is a limit to what even the meekest Christian can do.

You cannot control what others do or how they feel or react. On occasion it just isn't possible to be at peace with them—because *they* won't be at peace with *you*. This is the force of the phrase, "as far as it depends on you." You can exercise restraint, you can control yourself, you can do things which make for peace and harmony. Paul's point is that, if war is to exist, and on occasion it seems inevitable, be sure that it isn't *your* fault.

PUTTING THE PRINCIPLE INTO PRACTICE

If anyone seemed justified in "getting even," it was Jonathan Edwards, Puritan pastor in eighteenth-century Northampton, Massachusetts. In December 1748, Edwards told a man who applied for church membership that he must be born again before he could partake of the Lord's Supper. That sounds routine to us, but in eighteenth-century New England it was revolutionary. Up until Edwards took his stand, no profession of saving faith was required.

The opposition Edwards faced was hostile and vindictive. All that he asked was for an opportunity to explain his views from the pulpit. He even wrote a book on the subject. But the governing church council refused his request and few people even bothered to read his written defense.

The attack on Edwards was less theological than personal. But why? He hadn't committed adultery. He hadn't stolen money from the offering plate or slacked off in the preparation of his sermons. Perhaps no one has ever been *less* like a twentieth-century televangelist than this Puritan pastor! So why was he persecuted? Simply because he had the courage to suggest that the Bible restricted communion to those who were saved by grace through faith in Jesus Christ.

The burden Edwards carried became progressively more grievous, as seen in this letter he wrote to a friend:

> I need God's counsel in every step I take and every word I speak; as all that I do and say is watched by the multitude around me with the utmost strictness and with eyes of the greatest uncharitableness and severity, and let me do or say what I will, my words and actions are represented in dark colours, and the state of things is come to that, that they seem to think it greatly concerns them to blacken me and represent me in odious colours to the world to justify their own conduct—they seem to be sensible that now their character can't stand unless it be on the ruin of mine. They have publickly voted that they will have no more sacraments; and they have no way to justify themselves in that but to represent me as very bad. I therefore desire, dear sir, your fervent prayers to God. If He be for me, who can be against me? If He be with me, I need not fear ten thousands of the people. But I know myself unworthy of His presence and help, yet would humbly trust in His infinite grace and all sufficience.[5]

After a long and bitter dispute, Edwards was dismissed by his church on June 22, 1750. Rarely has a man been treated more unjustly than was Edwards. Yet he refused to strike back. One church member sympathetic to Edwards describes his pastor's reaction to being fired:

> That faithful witness received the shock, unshaken. I never saw the least symptoms of displeasure in his countenance the whole week, but he appeared like a man of God, whose happiness was out of the reach of his enemies and whose treasure was not only a future but a present good, overbalancing all imaginable ills of life, even to the astonishment of many who could not be at rest without his dismission.[6]

How was Edwards able to resist the urge to do what comes so easily for you and me? You just read the answer. His happiness, wrote Edwards's friend, "was out of the reach of his enemies."

Biographer Iain Murray points out that Edwards's farewell sermon leaves a vivid impression of his character. Says Murray, "He does not hide from his people that he had been plunged 'into an abyss of trouble and sorrow', yet his words are singularly free of blame or accusation."[7]

In this final message, mercy abounds. In this, his last official duty to his congregation, "it is *their* needs rather than his own which are uppermost in his mind as he longs that they and he, 'now parting one from another as to this world . . . may not be parted after our meeting at the last day'. No congregation was ever spoken to more tenderly than the people of Northampton on July 1, 1750."[8]

THE MARK OF MATURITY

Here, then, is genuine spiritual maturity. Here is meekness, without which mercy is stripped of its power. We see it in her who deals gently with those who resist. We see it in him who responds sensitively to those bent on abuse. We see it in the tender concern of a pastor for those who have maliciously robbed him of reputation and ministry.

So why do most of us score so poorly on the "meekness meter"? What is it about us that makes meekness, and therefore maturity, so incredibly elusive? Why are our best efforts so often spoiled by selfish concerns? We've already answered this question a dozen times, but it bears repeating. Larry Crabb says it this way:

> Within the heart of people lurks a deep fear that their longing to be treated as valuable may never be met. They cherish a fear of rejection and disrespect and feeling insignificant. A natural concern for personal safety prompts people to clothe themselves with emotional layers—protective coatings to shield themselves from insult and criticism, masks with which to greet each other, facades designed to prevent embarrassment or ridicule, contrived appearances which hide parts they find unacceptable.[9]

Self-protection, dear friend, is the mortal enemy of meekness. This is what it all boils down to. Either you are committed to your own emotional safety, with all the masks, facades, and contrived appearances that supply protection, or you are meek. You cannot be both. Self-protection leads to selfish manipulation of others, and retaliation when they fail to meet your demands. Meekness, on the other hand, enables you to bear their burdens, painful and inconvenient though it be.

Meekness will forever elude you until you embrace the fact that your security and significance are wrapped up in Christ, and not in the approval or acceptance of those to whom He has called you to minister. What was it again that Edwards's friend said of him? "His happiness was out of the reach of his enemies!"

So remember this. When your heart balks at humility and your flesh yearns for the satisfaction of settling a score, set your eyes on Jesus. He prayed for His enemies with every stroke of their hammer as they drove iron spikes into His hands and feet. If the horrors of crucifixion could not diminish the concern He had for His enemies, what possible excuse can you and I have?

Oh, by the way, meekness *does* have its rewards—just a few minor things like "the earth" (Matthew 5:5)!

ELEVEN

God's Second Greatest Gift

Just as each of us has one body with many members, and these members do not all have the same function, so in Christ we who are many form one body, and each member belongs to all the others. (Romans 12:4-5)

Now you are the Body of Christ, and each one of you is a part of it. (1 Corinthians 12:27)

Therefore each of you must put off falsehood and speak truthfully to his neighbor, for we are all members of one body. (Ephesians 4:25)

Some people just aren't the "joining" type. They stand aloof from the crowd. They rarely give much thought to membership in the Rotary Club or the YMCA or the Chamber of Commerce. They seem far more comfortable "on their own," without the obligations or the publicity that often come to those who join such organizations. Others are card-carrying members of any group that will have them! As long as the monthly dues aren't too steep, they'll sign up. I suppose it takes all kinds to make up this world of ours.

But when it comes to the Church, Christians don't have a choice. The Church is certainly not a club, nor even an organization. Nevertheless, from the moment we place our faith in the saving work of Jesus Christ we all become members of His Body (cf. 1 Corinthians 12:13). More than that, we become *members of one another.* That's not easy for Western individualists to understand. Joining the local country club is one thing, but how do you join another human being? What does membership in another person or group of persons mean?

LIFE IN THE BODY OF CHRIST

The authors of the New Testament, especially Paul, answer that question by means of analogy. Of all the metaphors used to illustrate the nature of the Church, that of a human body is the most frequent and most helpful. The Church, Paul explains, is like a body of which we are all members or parts or organs.

That's not too difficult to understand. After all, I know what it means to say "my body." I know what arms and legs and eyes and ears and toes and a nose are all about. I know that there is an obvious interdependence and mutual interaction in the function of my various bodily members. When I swing a golf club (alas, poorly), my right and left hands are each dependent on the other. It helps to have both eyes working "in sync" in order to read well. When my emotions are stirred I have chills down my back, and when I stub my toe my brain says "Ouch!"

That, says Paul, is what the Church is like. Individual believers are the arms and legs and livers and kneecaps of the Body of Christ! Each is in some way connected to the other. All are mutually interdependent. When my head itches my hand scratches. When my mouth eats too much my stomach pays the price. When my appendix ruptures my feet had better transport me quickly to the hospital. This need for cooperation is no less the case in the relationships between the various members of a local church.

This also means that injury to one part hurts all. The loss of a toe or ear can't help but impair the body as a whole. Earlier I described breaking my arm at the age of six. During that ordeal amputation became a frightening possibility. Not only had the elbow been shattered but there was extensive nerve damage as well. By God's grace and a physician's skill such radical steps proved unnecessary. It is difficult to imagine what my life would have been like without a left arm. Aside from the obvious discomfort, such a disability would certainly have restricted my activities as a young boy, and even as an adult.

The same principle applies in the local church. You and I and every other Christian are dependent upon and responsible to each other. The absence of one member directly affects the ability of the others to fulfill their God-given tasks.

The human body analogy accentuates how utterly ridiculous some of our attitudes and actions toward each other can be. As Jerry Bridges explains:

> Can you imagine the ear making the following comment to the eye? "Say, did you hear about the serious trouble the foot is having? My, my, isn't it too bad? That foot surely ought to get his act together." No, no, our bodies don't behave that way at all! Instead the entire body cries out, "My foot hurts! I feel awful!"
>
> Why does the whole body hurt when only one part is injured? It is because all the parts of the body make up one indivisible whole. And when one part hurts, no matter what the reason, the restorative powers of the entire body are brought to bear on that hurting member. Rather than attacking that suffering part or ignoring the problem, the rest of the body demonstrates concern for the part that hurts. This is the way the Body of Christ should function.[1]

This is what Paul meant in 1 Corinthians 12:25 when he said that *all* the parts of Christ's Body (you and I and everyone else), "should have equal concern for each other." This is the premise for all the many statements in the New Testament that contain the words "one another." Bearing one another's burdens is only one among literally dozens of obligations we have toward each other as fellow-members in the same spiritual body.

AN UNEXPECTED EXAMPLE

Every so often God provides an opportunity to bear someone's burden without our even knowing it.

One afternoon I received a call from a lady in our church. No sooner had Barbara spoken my name than I knew something was terribly wrong. She and her husband were confronted with a potentially disastrous financial and personal crisis. (Some like to think that faithful Christians will be spared such pain, but we know better.)

I rarely feel more inadequate as a Christian than when the phone rings like it did that day. Solid, spiritual advice doesn't come easily, yet the urge to say something profound is overwhelming. When I give in to it I usually make a mess of things. This time (thankfully) I resisted the temptation. There simply aren't any magical words that can make problems disappear. The last thing Barbara needed was for me to trivialize her anguish by spouting some religious cliché that sounded good but solved nothing.

That is why I was so surprised when she later told me how much help I'd been that day. "Really?" I said. "I don't remember saying anything especially powerful." Her explanation still astounds me. "Sam, after I had told you all that happened and how devastated I was, you asked me: 'Okay, so where do we go from here?' The simple fact that you said 'we' rather than 'you' seemed to ease the weight of my burden. More than anything else at that time I needed to know I wasn't alone. I just needed to know someone was going to face this with me."

Isn't grace amazing! God mercifully used *one word* to bolster the sagging spirits of His child. I don't recall having given much thought to my choice of words that day. But apparently the Holy Spirit did!

This wasn't a case of "misery loves company," as if Barbara thought by involving me in her pain the problem would vanish. It was simply another example of the Body of Christ fulfilling its divinely-ordained role wherein "if one part suffers, every part suffers with it" (1 Corinthians 12:26).

Only after an experience like that do Paul's words in Ephesians 4:16 really make sense: "From him the whole body, joined and held together by every supporting ligament, grows and builds itself up in love, as each part does its work." The process Paul describes has often been called "one-anothering."

THE SNARE OF SPIRITUAL SNOBBERY

There are, as you might guess, a lot of things that can stand in the way of "one-anothering." One in particular that I have found especially bothersome is *spiritual snobbery.* You can't very well minister to someone if you think you are "above that sort of thing," or worse yet, "above that sort of person."

"Do not be haughty in mind," wrote Paul to the Romans, "but associate with the lowly" (Romans 12:16, NASB). The word translated "lowly" may be either neuter or masculine in gender. If neuter, Paul may be referring to lowly tasks, menial chores, those responsibilities in the Church that call for humility and self-abnegation. But I'm inclined to believe he meant lowly *people.*

Paul is describing those who have nothing to offer us in return for our help, nothing with which to win the favor of the more powerful and sophisticated believers. The downcast, the disheartened, the deprived, and the social misfit are fellow members in the body no less so than "the rich and famous."

Paul could not have been more explicit. As John Murray put it, there must be "no aristocracy in the church, no cliques of the wealthy as over against the poor, no pedestals of unapproachable dignity for those on the higher social and economic strata or for those who are in office in the church."[2]

This was evidently a real problem in the churches to which James wrote his letter:

> My brothers, as believers in our glorious Lord Jesus Christ, don't show favoritism. Suppose a man comes into your meeting wearing a gold ring and fine clothes, and a poor man in shabby clothes also comes in. If you show special attention to the man wearing fine clothes and say, "Here's a good seat for you," but say to the poor man, "You stand there" or, "Sit on the floor by my feet," have you not discriminated among yourselves and become judges with evil thoughts? (James 2:1-4)

If we are not careful we might misunderstand what James is saying. He is not telling us to ignore the rich, as if they had no business being at church. Wealth itself does not disqualify anyone from the Kingdom of God. James is not suggesting that Christ died only for the poor. We must guard against reverse discrimination!

James wants us to treat all alike, without the slightest regard for socioeconomic factors. In other words, showing kindness and courtesy to wealthy visitors is not wrong. It is wrong only when we do it to curry their favor, or to the exclusion of the poor.

Let us also remember that, whereas James is denouncing that form of spiritual snobbery in which we cater to the rich, he could just as easily have denounced that *condescending humility* in which we falsely pity the poor. We must avoid both extremes. We should neither identify with the rich and look with disdain upon the poor nor identify with the poor and look with indignation upon the rich.

Furthermore, James did not intend to say that it is wrong to give honor to whom honor is due (cf. Philippians 2:29). It is by all means appropriate to acknowledge those who serve well the Body of Christ. His point, rather, is that we should not honor some to the dishonor of others, based solely on external, and especially economic, grounds.

Some have mistakenly thought that this passage forbids the rich from wearing their jewelry or fashionable clothes to church. That's about as ridiculous as insisting that the poor should deliberately dress ragged and dirty! I doubt that James could have cared less how people dressed, so long as they did so modestly and in good taste.

James's point is simply that, as long as you did not become poor because of sloth or rich because of deceit, your socioeconomic status is irrelevant in the eyes of God and should therefore be irrelevant in the eyes of the Church. Our "one-anothering" must never be selective. Your responsibility to others in the Body of Christ is neither enhanced nor diminished by the salary they draw or the educational degrees they have earned or the influence they wield in the community.

Today you can pretty much sit wherever you wish in most churches. But it wasn't always that way. Jonathan Edwards, of whom we read in chapter 10, was dismayed in 1737 when the church at Northampton erected a new building. Until that time, seating at their services had been based on such considerations as age, gender, social and military rank, and community service. (Most Christians today would find even that kind of policy somewhat distasteful.) But in 1737 several new criteria were introduced relating to a man's income and property holdings. Despite Edwards's protests, the wealthier citizens were given preferential seating while the poor were relegated to sitting in the gallery and back pews. That is hardly the sort of atmosphere that makes for mutual ministry and caring one for another!

I'm reminded of something I read about that happened during World War I. A Christian group opened a "rest house" for fellowship behind enemy lines. The goal was to welcome all, irrespective of military status. To make the point, a sign was placed over the entrance that read: "Abandon all rank, ye who enter here!" There are no privates or colonels or generals in the Body of Christ. We are all fellow-soldiers for the sake of the gospel.

SOME INSPIRED INSTRUCTIONS

Once we have cleared the hurdle of spiritual snobbery (which isn't to suggest we won't still stumble on occasion), we are prepared to do some serious one-anothering. It would be impossible for me to describe in detail the many one-anothering exhortations in the New Testament. Perhaps the most needful thing is for us simply to meditate prayerfully on the biblical imperatives themselves. Too much comment sometimes obscures the otherwise pristine clarity of the inspired text.

The most foundational one-anothering command is already familiar to you (see chapter 8). It is repeated several times in the New Testament:

> A new command I give you: Love one another. As I have loved you, so you must love one another. (John 13:34; cf. 15:12,17)

From this spiritual reservoir springs forth a veritable river of *one anothers*. Consider each of them carefully:

Salt is good; but if the salt becomes unsalty, with what will you make it salty again? Have salt in yourselves, and be at peace with one another. (Mark 9:50, NASB)

Be devoted to one another in brotherly love. (Romans 12:10)

Honor one another above yourselves. (Romans 12:10)

Live in harmony with one another. (Romans 12:16)

Therefore let us stop passing judgment on one another. (Romans 14:13)

So then let us pursue the things which make for peace and the building up of one another. (Romans 14:19, NASB)

Now may the God who gives perseverance and encouragement grant you to be of the same mind with one another according to Christ Jesus. (Romans 15:5, NASB)

Accept one another, then, just as Christ accepted you, in order to bring praise to God. (Romans 15:7)

You yourselves are . . . competent to instruct one another. (Romans 15:14)

Greet one another with a holy kiss. (Romans 16:16)

So then, my brethren, when you come together to eat, wait for one another. (1 Corinthians 11:33, NASB)

Serve one another in love. (Galatians 5:13)

But if you bite and devour one another, take care lest you be consumed by one another. (Galatians 5:15, NASB)

Let us not become boastful, challenging one another, envying one another. (Galatians 5:26, NASB)

Be completely humble and gentle; be patient, bearing with one another in love. (Ephesians 4:2)

Be kind and compassionate to one another, forgiving each other, just as in Christ God forgave you. (Ephesians 4:32)

Submit to one another out of reverence for Christ. (Ephesians 5:21)

Let each of you regard one another as more important than himself. (Philippians 2:3, NASB)

Do not lie to one another, since you laid aside the old self with its evil practices. (Colossians 3:9, NASB)

As those who have been chosen of God, holy and beloved, put on a heart of compassion, kindness, humility, gentleness and patience; bearing with one another, and forgiving each other. (Colossians 3:12-13, NASB)

Therefore comfort one another with these words. (1 Thessalonians 4:18, NASB)

Therefore encourage one another, and build up one another, just as you also are doing. (1 Thessalonians 5:11, NASB)

See that no one repays another with evil for evil, but always seek after that which is good for one another and for all men. (1 Thessalonians 5:15, NASB)

And let us consider how we may spur one another on toward love and good deeds. (Hebrews 10:24)

Brothers, do not slander one another. (James 4:11)

> Do not complain, brethren, against one another. (James 5:9, NASB)

> Therefore, confess your sins to one another, and pray for one another, so that you may be healed. (James 5:16, NASB)

> Offer hospitality to one another without grumbling. (1 Peter 4:9)

> Clothe yourselves with humility toward one another, because, "God opposes the proud but gives grace to the humble." (1 Peter 5:5)

To these scriptures I must add a word of warning: One-anothering can be hazardous to your health! You are entrusting yourself to untrustworthy people. Even Christians (some of you might wish I had said *especially* Christians) can be inconsiderate and ungrateful. The ingratitude and disloyalty of unbelievers is something we've come to expect. But it really hurts when the Body of Christ turns on itself.

Most of us know all too well what Solomon meant when he said, "Like a bad tooth or a lame foot is reliance on the unfaithful in times of trouble" (Proverbs 25:19). When we remember this was written before modern dentistry and the numbing effects of Novocaine, its force intensifies. Nothing is quite as irritating as chronic tooth pain. Nothing, that is, except for chronically unreliable and ungrateful "friends."

No one knew this better than the very man who issued most of those one-anothering commands. Paul must have had one doozy of a spiritual toothache as he wrote these words to young Timothy: "You know that *everyone* in the province of Asia has deserted me, including Phygelus and Hermogenes" (2 Timothy 1:15, emphasis added—although I think *he* wrote it emphatically as well!). Paul didn't need anyone to remind him of the words of Proverbs: "Many a man claims to have unfailing love, but a faithful man who can find?" (20:6).

Still, in the midst of his disappointment Paul rejoices in yet another man with a funny name (remember Epaphroditus?): "May the Lord show mercy to the household of Onesiphorus, because he often refreshed me and was not ashamed of my chains. On the contrary, when he was in Rome, he searched hard for me until he found me. May the Lord grant that he will find mercy from the Lord on that day! You know very well in how many ways he helped me in Ephesus" (2 Timothy 1:16-18).

All of us have known our own "Phygelus" and "Hermogenes." We've felt the pain of their personal abandonment. We've turned to them in a moment of crisis only to feel the cold blast of empty space. Thankfully, though, every so often we encounter an "Onesiphorus," that special someone who seemingly has every reason not to serve, but does anyway. People like Onesiphorus and Epaphroditus, funny names notwithstanding, are there to encourage us. They are also there to remind us that, if God's greatest gift is His Son *to us*, His second greatest gift is you and I—*to one another.*

TWELVE

The Arithmetic of Forgiveness

"Forgive as the Lord forgave you" (Colossians 3:13). It sounds simple enough. After all, it's only six words. Easy to read. Easy to memorize. But for some of us, virtually impossible to obey. Listen to it again: "Forgive as the Lord forgave you." To paraphrase a familiar saying, "Never has one man said so little to so many that demanded so much."

Will you agree with me that, of all the "one-anothering" tasks we listed in the previous chapter, *forgiving* one another is the toughest?

Let's be honest with each other: *grudges can be fun!*

We enjoy withholding forgiveness because it permits us to keep our enemies (and even some of our friends) under control. It gives us the opportunity to manipulate them into providing things we want from them. We use their offense against us as a rope to dangle them over the fires of vengeance. If we were to completely forgive them, we would lose our excuse for self-pity. And forgiveness would set them free from their obligation to us to "make good."

Few things cut across the grain of human nature like forgiving others. Breathing is easy. Eating is fun. No one thinks twice about blinking one's eyes. But forgiving others is sheer agony! It grates on our souls like fingernails on a chalkboard. King Louis XII of France spoke for us all when he said, "Nothing smells so sweet as the dead body of your enemy!"

JANET

Whenever I think about forgiveness, Janet comes to mind. She knows only too well both the pain and the power of forgiveness. But she didn't learn this at home. Her parents divorced when she was three, affording her precious little opportunity either to see in others or feel for herself the joy of love and acceptance.

Janet married for the first time when she was twenty. She wasn't prepared for the physical and emotional abuse her husband inflicted on her (is anyone?). Her first child, Randy, was born a year later. She and her husband separated when she was twenty-three and the divorce was finalized a little more than a year later. She married Mark shortly after that and insists their first four years together were reasonably happy ones.

Then, Janet became a Christian. At first Mark encouraged her. He, too, professed faith in Christ, but seemed reluctant to assume the responsibilities of a Christian husband.

Janet was like a sponge when it came to the Bible. Mark was more like a backboard. As time passed he seemed to resent Janet's spiritual growth and was uncomfortable with the depth of her dedication. Her manipulative attempts to change him were met with polite, but decisive, retreat. "Mark was *nice*," she said, "but consistently distant."

Meanwhile, her son Randy was becoming something of a problem. He had been hyper-active as a child and was now beginning to rebel. Mark was reluctant to admit that the problem was serious, and his failure to assist Janet in dealing with Randy's rebellion served only to widen the gap between them. Her expressions of concern were often met with an understanding smile and a quick exit to the office. Janet felt patronized, rejected, and even a bit betrayed.

Her efforts to find help from the church were disillusioning. "Somehow I got the message," she told me, "that *it was sub-Christian to admit you had problems*, especially in a church where the teaching of the Bible was paramount. I was told to 'pray about it' and 'turn it over to the Lord.' I sort of expected it all to work itself out in the end . . . like a television sit-com. Certainly there was no need to involve anyone else in my problems."

Then Mark lost his job. With their move to another town Randy got worse. Problems at school were on the increase. Discipline was ineffective. Janet suspected drugs. She was right.

Following another job-change for Mark and another move, Randy ran away from home. He was in and out of drug rehabilitation programs, juvenile detention centers, and eventually jail. Janet's sense of failure as a mother was aggravated by deepening feelings of rejection. Again, Mark lost his job. Again, another move.

It wasn't unusual for Janet to cry herself to sleep, doubled over with pain and loneliness. It wasn't so much that Mark didn't want to help. He didn't know how. He was always kind and courteous, never abusive. But they continued to drift apart. The intimacy of married life had all but died.

One thing you must understand about Janet is that she never once abandoned hope in the Lord Jesus Christ. Her theological roots went deep into God's Word, and she found her solace in the glorious truth of God's sovereign grace.

But the pain was still there. The anger and bitterness and feelings of betrayal didn't vanish into thin air when she became a believer. Somehow she had to confront the reality of rejection and deal with the resentment in her heart. Her wounds went deep into the soul; she needed healing.

My reason for telling you about Janet is to provide a point of contact. Many of us know what she's been through, having experienced it ourselves. We can identify with her pain and her predicament. You may be wondering if strained relationships can ever be restored, or if the joy of salvation will ever return.

At least in Janet's case, the answer is a heartening and resounding *yes!* I am delighted to tell you that the chains of bitterness have been broken and her oppressive burden has begun to lighten. Mark has repented and daily deepens in his love for both his Savior and his wife. Janet and Mark have a long way to go, but they are, perhaps for the first time, growing in grace together.

What happened? To come straight to the point, Janet learned the lesson Jesus taught Peter in Matthew 18:21-35. She learned the lesson of forgiveness.

THE INTERROGATION

> Then Peter came and said to Him, "Lord, how often shall my brother sin against me and I forgive him? Up to seven times?" Jesus said to him, "I do not say to you, up to seven times, but up to seventy times seven." (verses 21-22, NASB)

The rabbis in the first century had agreed that a brother or sister should be forgiven up to three times, but on the fourth offense no forgiveness was required. Perhaps Peter fancied himself big-hearted by volunteering to go beyond what the religious leaders of his day had taught. He may even have hoped to impress Jesus with his magnanimous and expansive spirit.

Clearly, though, Peter was thinking like a legalist. He thought mercy was something you could measure. He thought compassion was something you could count. Jesus shattered his thinking: "I tell you, not seven times, but seventy times seven!"

Don't get the idea that Jesus meant 490 and not one more! He was not suggesting that you need to be patient until your brother sins against you for the 491st time, at which moment you are free to punch him in the nose! He simply picked up on Peter's number and multiplied it by ten and then again by seven, as His way of indicating a number that for all practical purposes is beyond computation.

People living under law might keep records, but not those governed by grace. We must be prepared to forgive the one-hundredth and the one-thousandth sin against us with the same zeal and sincerity as we do the first. Jesus makes the same point in Luke 17:3-4 where He says, "If your brother sins, rebuke him, and if he repents, forgive him. If he sins against you seven times in a day, and seven times comes back to you and says, 'I repent,' forgive him."

THE ILLUSTRATION

Peter must have been stunned by what Jesus said. But it doesn't stop there. Jesus goes on to illustrate His point.

"Therefore, the kingdom of heaven is like a king who wanted to settle accounts with his servants. As he began the settlement, a man who owed him ten thousand talents was brought to him. Since he was not able to pay, the master ordered that he and his wife and his children and all that he had be sold to repay the debt. The servant fell on his knees before him. 'Be patient with me,' he begged, 'and I will pay back everything.' The servant's master took pity on him, canceled the debt and let him go.

"But when that servant went out, he found one of his fellow servants who owed him a hundred denarii. He grabbed him and began to choke him. 'Pay back what you owe me!' he demanded. His fellow servant fell to his knees and begged him, 'Be patient with me, and I will pay you back.' But he refused. Instead, he went off and had the man thrown into prison until he could pay the debt. When the other servants saw what had happened, they were greatly distressed and went and told their master everything that had happened.

"Then the master called the servant in. 'You wicked servant,' he said, 'I canceled all that debt of yours because you begged me to. Shouldn't you have had mercy on your fellow servant just as I had on you?' In anger his master turned him over to the jailers to be tortured, until he should pay back all he owed.[1]

"This is how my heavenly Father will treat each of you unless you forgive your brother from your heart." (Matthew 18:23-35)

Ten thousand talents was an enormous sum of money. Some have estimated that it would translate into approximately $12 million by today's monetary standards. Just to give you an idea of this man's debt, the entire tax payment from the provinces of Galilee and Perea in the year Jesus was born amounted to only two hundred talents. The yearly income of King Herod was but nine hundred talents. If this man were to work one thousand weeks he could only earn (much less save) one talent!

Clearly, it would be impossible for him to pay such a debt.

Jesus knew this. He deliberately exaggerated the size of the debt to emphasize how utterly hopeless was the man's plight.

A remarkable element in this story is that the king, who obviously represents God, does not do what the man requests . . . he does far more. The man asks that he be given time and opportunity to repay the debt. But the king says, "That will not be necessary. I release you from the debt altogether; I forgive you *everything*!"

Notwithstanding this incomprehensible display of mercy, the man refuses to release a fellow-servant whose debt is approximately one-six-thousandth the size of his own! The disproportion magnifies how bizarre and unthinkable the servant's behavior is. Worse yet, the words of the second servant ["Be patient with me, and I will pay you back"] should have evoked compassion in the heart of the first, reminding him of the very words he had spoken to the king.

Jesus' point can hardly be missed: In view of the debt of sin God has forgiven us (indeed, our case was utterly hopeless as well), how dare we refuse to forgive a brother or sister whose debt is by comparison a mere trifle.

The principle is one we must hear well. Our forgiving others is the gracious overflow of God's having forgiven us! This is the lesson Janet learned. It is what made the difference in her life and especially in her relationship with Mark. She once said to me: "How dare I not forgive others, having been forgiven so much myself? My sins put Jesus on the tree. What right do I have to withhold forgiveness from those who in turn have sinned against me? Ephesians 4:32 kept haunting my mind: 'Be kind and compassionate to one another, forgiving each other, just as in Christ God forgave you.'"

A PROMISE NOT TO REMEMBER

What is forgiveness anyway? Thus far I've used the term freely without defining it. Most of us think we have an idea of what forgiveness means but it usually turns out to be a pathetic facsimile of the real thing.

Jay Adams has suggested that our definition should come

from God. After all, we are to forgive others "just as" God forgave us. Well, then, how *did* God forgive us? When God forgave us in Christ Jesus, what did He do?

According to the terms of the "new covenant" foretold in Jeremiah 31, God said, "For I will forgive their wickedness and will remember their sins no more" (verse 34; cf. Isaiah 43:25). In other words, God has remarkably gone on record with a promise *not to remember* our sins anymore.

But if God is omniscient, how can He "forget" our sins? He can't. But then the text doesn't say God "forgets" our sins. It says He promises "not to remember" them. That is not just playing with words. Adams explains:

> Obviously, the omniscient God who created and sustains the universe does not forget, but He can "not remember." You see, forgetting is passive and is something that we human beings, not being omniscient, do. "Not remembering" is active; it is a promise whereby one person (in this case, God) determines not to remember the sins of another *against him*. To "not remember" is simply a graphic way of saying, "I will not bring up these matters to you or others in the future. I will bury them and not exhume the bones to beat you over the head with them. I will never use these sins against you."[2]

When we apply this to our relationship with others, the following definition emerges: "When you say, 'I forgive you' to another, you make a promise to him. It is a threefold promise. You promise not to remember his sin by not bringing it up to him, to others, or to yourself. The sin is buried."[3]

And what about "forgetting"? Well,

> When you make the promise to not remember one's sins against him anymore and keep it, you will find that you will forget! Indeed, the very best way to forget is to keep the promise. If you don't rehearse the wrongdoing to others or to yourself, more quickly than you'd realize it will fade away. Forgiving is the only way to forget![4]

One more observation about the mercy of forgiveness is in order. *True forgiveness leads to loving involvement.* As much as the other person will permit it, you and I must become personally involved in their life. "Forgiveness," Adams reminds us, "is not an end in itself; it is a means to an end—a new and better relationship with those from whom we have become estranged."[5]

If we do not *pursue* the person whom we forgive, our promise not to remember their sin against us can easily degenerate into a hypocritical, self-serving form of manipulation. The test of our sincerity is the lengths to which we are willing to go in ministering to this person's need.

Often we do wish we could forget after we forgive: we wish we could forget *the person we forgave*! There are occasions when we don't want anything to do with that person beyond what is absolutely necessary. "Good-bye and good riddance! I never liked her in the first place." What this attitude reveals is our tendency to pervert forgiveness into an excuse for washing our hands of someone we don't like. We want to be rid of their annoying presence, and forgiveness seems to provide us with "a good out."

As we have noted, if the forgiven person is still an unwanted person, our supposed forgiveness is nothing more than manipulation. It becomes little more than a tool by which we satisfy our own needs rather than serve the other person. True forgiveness, on the other hand, is a ministry of mercy. It is a responsibility that should thrust us into the life of the forgiven person, to give and to serve and to sacrifice to the same extent to which Christ Jesus gave and served and sacrificed Himself for us.

FORGIVE AS THE LORD FORGAVE YOU

If ever Jesus needed a friend, this was the time. Earlier in His ministry Jesus had often wanted to be alone. He would quietly slip away while the others were sleeping, hungry for solitude, for that rare moment alone with the Father, away from the pressure of the crowds and the endless questioning of the Pharisees.

That was then. This was now . . . the night of His betrayal. "This very night," said Jesus, "you will all fall away on account of me" (Matthew 26:31). Not just any night, but "this very night," the night Jesus and the disciples sat together in the upper room and enjoyed a depth of personal and spiritual intimacy perhaps unlike anything they had known before. "This very night," said Jesus, "the night we ate together, prayed together, sang together. . . ."

"You will be offended by me," Jesus told them. "Your faith will turn to fear. At first sight of the enemy you will all turn tail and scamper away into the shadows like so many frightened pups. . . . For it is written, 'I will strike the shepherd, and the sheep of the flock will be scattered'" (verse 31).

"Not me, Lord! No way!" Peter's protest was loud and arrogant. "Maybe John will abandon You. I mean, anyone so loving has to be a little soft, a bit weak, especially when the chips are down. But not me! Not good old Peter! Hey, don't forget, Lord, I'm the 'Rock!' You said so Yourself. Remember?"

"Peter, let me tell you something . . ." Jesus replied: "This very night before the rooster crows, you will disown me three times" (verse 34).

But once again, Peter boldly begged to differ with Jesus. We can only imagine what more he might have said, or at least thought, in reaction to the dire prediction about him: "I hear you, Lord. And I don't mean to sound argumentative. But I'll never disown you. I'll die first! I can't speak for the others. Some of them aren't as strong as I am. They didn't walk on water like me. Sure, I know you selected each of them, Lord, but don't forget that Matthew there was a tax-collector. It wouldn't surprise me to see him revert to his former ways. And I grew up with Andrew. If you only knew how often he's messed up. But not me, Lord. You can count on old Peter!"

Instead of falling on his face and humbly pleading for gracious enablement to withstand the coming test, Peter implicitly accused Jesus of lying. But he wasn't alone in this, for "all the other disciples said the same" (verse 35). We don't know what motivated them to chime in with Peter's protest. Perhaps they were sincere, or maybe they just didn't want to be outdone by Peter's declaration of love and loyalty.

In any case, Jesus was right and they were wrong. That doesn't surprise you, does it? Following His arrest in Gethsemane, "all the disciples deserted him and fled" (verse 56).

But wait a minute. *Maybe Peter really meant what he said.* We're told that Peter, "followed him at a distance, right up to the courtyard of the high priest. He entered and sat down with the guards to see the outcome" (verse 58).

What could Peter possibly have been thinking? Had he forgotten Jesus' prediction? It had only been a few hours before. Was it already a fading memory? Or was he still puffed up with confidence in his own power to resist, determined to prove his Lord wrong?

The kangaroo court convened. Trumped-up charges. Lying witnesses. Accusations of blasphemy. And then the consummate indignity: "They spit in his face and struck him with their fists. Others slapped him and said, 'Prophesy to us, Christ. Who hit you?'" (verses 67-68).

And where was Peter when Jesus needed him most? He "was sitting out in the courtyard, and a servant girl came to him. 'You also were with Jesus of Galilee,' she said" (verse 69).

Finally, Peter probably said to himself, *the time has come for me to prove my point and show everyone what I'm made of. At last, the opportunity to demonstrate how deep my loyalty runs.*

Well, not quite: "But he denied it before them all. 'I don't know what you're talking about,' he said" (verse 70). It was a standoff: Peter, the Rock, the strong-armed, grizzled fisherman, face-to-face with . . . with . . . a "servant girl"? Surely not! Had Peter been confronted by Pontius Pilate and threatened with immediate execution perhaps we might understand (though by no means excuse) his failure. If it were Caiaphas, the high priest, or Annas, or a Roman soldier with a sword pressed perilously close to his throat, . . . but a "servant girl"? John Calvin was right:

> Here we see that it does not take a heavy fight to break a man, nor many forces and devices. Whoever is not dependent on God's hand will soon fall, at a breath of wind or the noise of a falling leaf. Peter certainly was no less brave than any of us, and had already given no ordinary proof of his high courage (though his boldness was excessive). Yet he does not wait to be brought to the tribunal of the Pontiff, or until the enemy threatens his violent death, but, at the

> voice of a young woman, he is scared, and straight out denies his Master.[6]

Frustrated and fearful, Peter sought an avenue of escape. He went out to the gateway but was again confronted, this time by . . . you guessed it, "another girl" (Matthew 26:71)! She said to the people there, "This fellow was with Jesus of Nazareth" (verse 71). But Peter "denied it again, with an oath: 'I don't know the man!'" (verse 72).

Peter didn't use profanity, as some have thought. His oath was in all likelihood an appeal to something sacred—used to reinforce the truth of his denial. Perhaps he said, "By all that is holy, I swear I don't know the man!" Or, "With God as my witness, this man is a stranger to me!"

When challenged yet a third time, "he began to call down curses on himself and he swore to them, 'I don't know the man!'" (verse 74). Peter not only invoked a solemn curse on himself should he be lying, but also upon his accusers should they persist in bringing such charges against him.

Adding insult to injury, he even refused to use the name of Jesus. He contemptuously and disdainfully refers to Him as "the man." How far he had fallen from that monumental confession: "You are the Christ, the Son of the living God" (Matthew 16:16).

Let's be clear about one thing. My detailed portrayal of Peter's sin is not designed to hold him up for public ridicule. I understand all too well Peter's weakness. Don't we all? Why, then, have I gone to such lengths to describe his cowardice? The answer is found in something only Luke of the four gospel authors records.

All four writers record the crowing of the rooster. The beloved physician alone tells us that at the precise moment of Peter's third denial, just as the rooster crowed, "the Lord turned and looked straight at Peter" (Luke 22:61). Peter's loud cursing still echoed in the courtyard of Caiaphas when Jesus looked . . . and their eyes locked! "Then Peter remembered the word the Lord had spoken to him: 'Before the rooster crows today, you will disown me three times.' And he went outside and wept bitterly" (verses 61-62).

When Jesus turned and looked at Peter He saw an angry and defiant man, a man whose adamant declarations of undying allegiance had withered at the sound of a servant girl's voice.

What did Peter see? Into what kind of eyes did he gaze? On what kind of face did he look? Was it the face of a well-groomed yuppie? Was it the face of a freshly washed, neatly manicured businessman? Was it the face of a nicely shaved, nattily attired politician?

I'll tell you what Peter saw. He looked into blackened eyes, virtually closed from the beating Jesus had endured. Bruised cheeks, swollen jaw, bloodied nose, with the vile and venomous spittle of His taunters dripping from His beard.

Peter looked with horror at the face of Jesus. With what did Jesus look back at Peter?

There are all sorts of "looks." Our eyes alone can communicate virtually every human emotion. There is the flirtatious look that passes between two teens in the hallways at school. There is the intimidating stare of two boxers in the middle of the ring.

There are the "looks that kill," the looks that pass between two people after one has abandoned and betrayed the other.

There is the "I-told-you-so" look, that unmistakable facial contortion reminding one of past failures and broken promises. It is a condescending glare, a look of smug superiority.

The look of anger is one we all know well. No words are necessary, only a disdainful sneer that says, "Some friend you turned out to be! Where were you when I needed you most?"

We've all been on the receiving (and sending) end of the look of resentment. I'm talking about one of those "after-all-I've-done-for-you-this-is-what-I-get-in-return" looks.

Perhaps the most painful look of all is the one of disappointment. Combined with a sad shaking of the head it says, "You sorry, no-good bum. I should have expected something like this from someone like you."

But how did Jesus look at Peter?

Was it with disdain or disappointment or anger or resentment? I don't think so. I wasn't there. I can only speculate. Neither Matthew nor Mark nor Luke nor John tells us. But I think I know.

I think Jesus turned toward Peter with a look that he recognized immediately, a look of incredible power, enough to bring down the stone barriers of a military fortress. In this case it pierced the sinful walls of Peter's stricken heart. Peter remembered . . .

and he went outside and wept bitterly.

So what did he see in those bruised and bloodied eyes? Unspoken words: "It's okay, Peter. It really is okay. I still love you as much now as I ever did before. It's okay." It was more than Peter could believe. After what he had done, knowing what he deserved, the eyes of Jesus said, "I forgive you."

Make no mistake about the pain Jesus felt in hearing Peter's denial. It isn't totally unlike the pain you and I feel when we're abandoned by those on whom we counted. Our trust in others is betrayed. We find ourselves all alone, with nothing but the echo of empty promises and unfulfilled pledges. When we've needed someone most, we hear only their words of rejection. In place of a friend we get a foe, instead of a companion we find a coward.

What kind of look do we communicate to those who treat us, in our hour of need, like Peter treated Jesus in His?

"Forgive as the Lord forgave you." Fine. But just how is it that the Lord has forgiven you? That's easy. Think of Peter's lapse. Now think of Jesus' look. That's how.

But this was not the end of the story for Peter! There came another opportunity for Peter to make known how he felt about Jesus. This time, though, he wasn't interrogated by a servant girl, but by the risen Lord Himself. Only the mercy of forgiveness, embodied in that one momentary look, can account for the difference between three angry denials and three affirmations of love:

> When they had finished eating, Jesus said to Simon Peter, "Simon son of John, do you truly love me more than these?" "Yes, Lord," he said, "you know that I love you." Jesus said, "Feed my lambs." Again Jesus said, "Simon son of John, do you truly love me?" He answered, "Yes, Lord, you know that I love you." Jesus said, "Take care of my sheep." The third time he said to him, "Simon son of John, do you love me?" Peter was hurt because Jesus asked him the third time, "Do you love me?" He said, "Lord, you know all things; you know that I love you." Jesus said, "Feed my sheep." (John 21:15-17)

"Forgive as the Lord forgave you."

THIRTEEN

Mercy in Practice

Jackie Pullinger was only five years old when she first sensed the call of God on her life. As she grew to adulthood the message became even more clear: "Go."

"Where, Lord?"

"Go, trust Me, and I will lead you."

Rebuffed and turned down by every missionary organization she contacted (no one wanted a British musician who lacked proper "missiological" training), Jackie sought the advice of her pastor. "Well, if you've tried all the conventional ways and missionary societies and God still is telling you to go, you had better get on the move. . . . If I were you I would go out and buy a ticket for a boat going on the longest journey you can find and pray to know where to get off."[1]

She did. Jackie Pullinger quite literally took "a slow boat to China," and for the past twenty-five years has been *doing mercy* in Hong Kong.

The infamous Walled City, where Jackie set up shop, sits on only six-and-one-half acres of land but is "home" for upwards of 50,000 people! It is quite literally a world unto itself, with neither China nor Great Britain exercising proper jurisdiction. It is a haven for thieves, murderers, extortionists, drug lords, illegal immigrants and refugees, the homeless, runaways, pimps, and prostitutes (many of whom were twelve- and thirteen-year-old girls, sold into the trade by neighbors, boyfriends, even parents).

Pornographic theaters, as well as opium and heroin dens, lined the narrow walkways and alleys. The city was ruled by the Triads, Chinese secret societies that had degenerated into ruthless criminal gangs.

The filth is beyond belief. Open sewers, refuse flowing freely in the streets, rats that no longer react to the shrill screams of frightened visitors. Bodies of addicts who overdosed the night before are piled outside the city.

Into this nightmare walked a twenty-year-old girl from England who knows something about mercy. Jackie began to tell the heroin addicts about Jesus. She spoke of divine love to prostitutes. She fed the hungry, provided shelter for the homeless, clothed the naked, and through God's power healed the sick.

And how did those she helped respond to her mercy? They broke into the Youth Club she'd opened and destroyed everything in sight. Tables and chairs were smashed, windows were broken, and the walls were smeared with excrement. When one of the drug lords, Goko, discovered that his men were responsible, he ordered them to go back and apologize.

They protested, "But she will never forgive us or welcome us back after what we did."

"She has to," Goko replied, "she's a Christian."

During the past twenty-five years God has used Jackie Pullinger to deliver hundreds of men and women from drug addiction; and their deliverance is pain-free, without any agony of withdrawal. People who for ten, twenty, even thirty years, had injected heroin directly into their veins have been set free through the power of the Holy Spirit.

Some of you may be overwhelmed by the ministry of Jackie Pullinger. You may think that her story is out of place in a book such as this. After all, the vast majority of people who read *To Love Mercy* are middle-class Americans who will never see the likes of a Walled City, or the depths of depravity it housed.

That's true. But mercy is the same all over the world. You don't have to go to Hong Kong or to Bangladesh or to Soweto in order to answer the call of God on your life (unless, of course, that is where God has called you). The sick, the hungry, the fearful, the depressed, the enslaved, the needy, the outcast, the confused, the hopeless, and the helpless are next door, across the street, in the pew next to you at church.

Mercy, I've come to discover, is like milk. If it sits unused too long, it spoils. Mercy was made to be used. It isn't like a gold-plated trophy, tucked away on a bookshelf gathering dust, serving only to remind us of what once was or of some past achievement. Mercy must always be on the move. Inert mercy is a contradiction in terms, like "fried snow." Like a muscle, mercy atrophies if not exercised.

If God had opted merely to sit in Heaven "emoting" mercy as He looked down on the wretched condition of His creation, none of us would be where we are now. None of us would be what we are now, His children. Yes, God "felt" mercy. But that feeling was merely a prelude to His taking gracious action on our behalf (cf. Ephesians 2:4-5). God's decision to show mercy was costly. It came at the expense of His own dear Son.

A church may be filled to the rafters with men and women who understand the concepts in this book and have come to grips with their longings and self-protective agendas. But nothing will change nor will Christ be glorified until we humble ourselves before God and start *doing* mercy.

As our study draws to a close, let's look at some concrete ways to do mercy. What shape does mercy take on, in a local church? What does it look like? There are countless books on the subject of ministry, service, the use of spiritual gifts, and so on. I see no need for repeating their conclusions here. Permit me to make a few observations that may at first seem overly simple, perhaps even routine.

AN AGENDA FOR PRACTICING MERCY

Being a pastor, I want to begin with pastors and others in positions of church leadership. What can *we* do?

We can start by admitting that we are the ones largely responsible for creating an atmosphere in which those who most need mercy are too intimidated to receive it! Those who could profit most from the comfort and encouragement of the Body of Christ often stay away, having been made to feel unworthy to mix with

Christians who seem to have it all together. Frequently the message they hear and see runs something like this: "Get your life in order! Dress in style! Smile all the time! And whatever you do, don't let on that you have any problems! Then, and only then, will you be worthy of receiving what our 'fellowship' has to offer!"

That isn't a message anyone actually preaches. Thank God for that! But people hear it nonetheless. How? Where? From whom? Ask yourself these questions and see if an answer doesn't emerge.

What is the composition of your church board and committees? Are they dominated by professional people? Lawyers? Physicians? Those with a college or even post-graduate education? I'm not suggesting these people are disqualified. I have some on my board. But where in the New Testament is any such factor a requirement for service? Some of the best and brightest and most mature Christians I know barely finished high school and buy their clothes at second-hand stores.

With whom do you mingle before and after the Sunday service? Who is invited to your home for dinner? What kind of people are entrusted with responsibility for church activities? Do you see a pattern, a kind of socioeconomic sameness?

What can be done about this? We can start by being a source of instruction and encouragement to *everyone* in our churches who might want to become "active mercy givers." Ideally all Christians, as they are moved by the Holy Spirit, should take the initiative in showing mercy. But we don't live in an ideal world, nor in an ideal church. We may not like it, but the fact remains that people will pursue what the pastor publicly endorses and encourages. Few Christians are sufficiently mature and motivated to undertake a ministry without the approval and support of those who are over them in the Lord.

It isn't enough, though, for pastors merely to talk about mercy from the pulpit. The "Preach and Retreat" approach won't inspire anyone to anything except passivity. Personal pastoral involvement is essential. Pastor, elder, deacon, Sunday-school teacher, *you* must do mercy. Put some teeth to your teaching by obeying your own advice! After we have exhorted and encouraged let us be diligent, says the Apostle Peter, to be "examples" to the flock (1 Peter 5:3).

What can you do? Start with something simple, like saying hello to that social pariah in your fellowship whose eyes everyone conveniently avoids lest they be drawn into an uncomfortable conversation. Put out a little extra effort to cross a crowded room to shake the hand that others cringe at the thought of touching. Dare even to hug that person who is convinced that no one could possibly care enough to acknowledge they exist. You will be surprised to discover how many in your church think they aren't "worth" the pastor's time. Prove them wrong.

Church leaders who pass pleasantries only because it's their job are a cancer in their own congregations. That sort of ecclesiastical hypocrisy will undermine everything you preach. Here's a suggestion. Each week select one person, or perhaps one family, to spend time with, if only on Sunday morning. Seek them out. Gently inquire into their circumstances. Make them feel special, not as a formality but because they *are* special. Speak with them undistracted by goings-on around you. Make it clear that as far as you are concerned no one else in the room matters, because at *that* moment no one else does! Engage them as if their questions and concerns were at that time the most pressing issue in *your* life.

Simply put, commit yourself to creating an atmosphere in which showing mercy and loving the unlovely is both easy and natural.

Here are several things that all of us can do. There's nothing especially profound about them, but they aren't for that reason any less important. You may think such deeds pale in comparison with the work Jackie Pullinger is doing in Hong Kong, but I'm not so sure.

1. *Begin with confession and repentance.* A prayer we could probably all pray is this:

> Most merciful heavenly Father,
>
> I confess and acknowledge that my commitment has been less to serving Jesus than to protecting myself. My dedication to personal soul-safety has come at great expense to others who may have needed my help. I have worshiped at the altar of convenience, isolation, and self-image. I have

neglected ministry and the service of Your people. I have been controlled by the fear of man rather than the fear of God. Most merciful heavenly Father, forgive me.

2. *Go to those whom you have failed and ask for their forgiveness* (cf. Matthew 5:23-26, James 5:16). Tell them of specific occasions when you *knew* they needed your gracious and merciful assistance but you chose for selfish reasons to shut your eyes to their predicament.

Well, of course it's going to hurt! But honesty is the only thing that will convince them you *do* care. It is the only thing that will overcome their understandable resistance and grant you access back into their life.

3. *Don't try to tackle too much too soon.* Select one person or one act of mercy or one opportunity each week and make him/her/it the exclusive focus of your energies. Don't be put off or rationalize yourself into inactivity by the magnitude of needs that exist. God doesn't expect from you more than what He has equipped you to accomplish. There is a wealth of healing mercy in such little things as:

- ◆ a well-timed phone-call just to say, "I care and I'm here if you need me";
- ◆ a card or brief letter that reminds the person who thinks she isn't worth remembering that she really is;
- ◆ an invitation to lunch or coffee, nothing fancy, but enough that he knows someone enjoys his company;
- ◆ a visit to the hospital during your lunch break (where is it written that only pastors do this?);
- ◆ a visit to the nursing home; you have no idea how lonely they really are;
- ◆ take aside in the hall of the church that person you know is hurting and pray with them; don't part company with an "I'll pray for you" promise (the Christian equivalent of "Have a nice day"); pray with them *right then and there* (can you imagine what our churches would be like if people really did pray for one another *right then and there*!);
- ◆ take it upon yourself to greet people at the entrance to

the church; if they are visitors, answer their questions, give them directions to the nursery, find them a good seat up front (even if they aren't dressed "appropriately," and then *you* go and sit with them!);

◆ keep your eye out for those who consistently slip into church unnoticed, walk close to the wall, and sit secluded and silently; Christ died for them too!

4. *Make a point of looking up those whose absence from church on Sunday has become more than sporadic.* Contact them, not for the purpose of passing judgment or humiliating them, but to communicate your genuine concern for their welfare and your interest and willingness to help in whatever problem accounts for their having been away.

5. *Focus especially on the needs, hurts, and fears of those who have no internal familial support.* This would include widows, orphans, the elderly, and single mothers (especially the divorced, who invariably see themselves as moral lepers in today's Church). If a benevolence fund does not exist in the church to assist them, start one.

6. *Let people know you are available.* Few will risk seeking your help if you haven't first made it clear that you are happy to give it. No one wants to be guilty of imposing where they aren't welcome.

7. *Prepare yourself for rejection.* Most people are reluctant at first to respond to overtures of mercy from someone who in the past has related from a posture of self-serving hypocrisy. It takes time. Only after repeated efforts, repeated rebuffs, only after they are persuaded that you are motivated by something other than self-righteousness will they open the door of their lives to your ministry.

8. *Get involved in a small-group Bible study or support fellowship.* If there isn't one in your church, start one! Visit your local Christian bookstore and ask for material on small-group ministry.

9. *The church that has truly been gripped with the reality of divine mercy will be busily ministering to the needs of two groups of people: the sexually abused and the physically disabled.* I can't begin to outline the details required for effective ministry to each;

others have done a marvelous job at that. My desire is simply to alert you to the need.

If the statistics I read are accurate, as many as four of every ten women in *your* church fellowship were sexually abused before the age of eighteen. You may feel helpless in the face of something like this, but there are three things you can do:

- First, work at creating an atmosphere of acceptance that will convince the victim of abuse she has nothing to fear by revealing her secret.
- Second, educate yourself on the subject so that you will be prepared to understand her anguish and the source of her self-loathing.
- Third, push for the creation of a support group in which victims of abuse can learn to draw from the experience and compassion of those who have suffered in like fashion.

And what of the physically disabled? In a society that measures personal worth by physical beauty and athletic achievement, such people face innumerable obstacles. I can here only recommend two courses of action:

- First, make contact with the ministry of Joni Eareckson Tada. Information is available by writing her at Joni and Friends, P. O. Box 3333, Agoura Hills, CA 91301.
- In the meantime, it doesn't take much effort to ensure that your church's physical plant is accessible to the disabled. If it isn't, volunteer your time and money to make it so.

A FRENCH FABLE[2]

One of my favorite folk tales will serve as a fitting climax to this chapter. It reveals the heart of a true servant:

> Once upon a time, a king had a servant who was known throughout the realm for his hard work and ministry to others. One day the servant took some rare time off, left the

castle, and wandered into the woods. There he stumbled into a shady glen where he discovered a genie, sitting on a rock and holding a lamp in his hands.

"Good day, most faithful servant," said the genie. "I have heard of you and the work you do for others. I have been waiting for this moment. Since you have labored so diligently on behalf of others, the time has come for you to enjoy yourself. With this magic lamp I can grant you one wish. Make your choice carefully, for I can answer only one request."

Without hesitating the servant responded, "I don't want to serve anymore. From now on I want to *be* served. I want to give the orders, not take them."

When the servant returned to the castle he immediately discovered that his wish had been granted. The guard opened the door for him. Men and women rushed to fulfill his every command. They cooked for him, cleaned for him, worked for him. Even his former master, the king, was at his beck and call.

At first, the man was delighted. But soon he became annoyed. After three months of being served, he could stand no more. He rushed to the woods and frantically searched for the genie. He said, "I've found out that I don't like to be idle and have others serve me. I want my old job back. I want once again to be the servant of others."

The genie answered, "I'm sorry. Don't you remember when I told you that I had power to grant you only one wish? I can't help you."

"But you don't understand," the man cried. "I've discovered that serving others is far better than having others serve me. Please help me. I'd rather be in *hell* than not be able to serve other people."

"Dear friend," said the genie, "where do you think you've been for the last three months?"

FOURTEEN

"*Blessed Are the Merciful*"

Several years ago I had the opportunity to see Francis Schaeffer's film series *How Should We Then Live?* I also read his book by the same title. Among the many perceptive observations Schaeffer made about Western civilization, one in particular has stuck with me. He concluded that the majority of people in our society have adopted two impoverished values: *Personal peace* and *affluence.*

We all know what affluence is, but it was his definition of personal peace that most captured my attention. "Personal peace," wrote Schaeffer, "means just to be let alone, not to be troubled by the troubles of other people, whether across the world or across the city—to live one's life with minimal possibilities of being personally disturbed."[1]

What makes this so tragic is that it isn't a cherished value merely of the nonChristian majority, but of many in the Church as well. People just don't want to be bothered. Ministry is too messy, too time-consuming, too entangling. "I've got enough problems of my own without having to worry about someone else. Just leave me alone!" Heard it before? Chances are you'll hear it again.

But not from Jesus.

JESUS AND MERCY

Our Lord looked at things a bit differently. In fact, the people He considered most blessed were the very ones society scorns and avoids. "Blessed are the meek," He said, "for they will inherit the earth" (Matthew 5:5). "Blessed are the poor in spirit, for theirs is the kingdom of heaven" (5:3). Gentleness, spiritual poverty, a hunger for righteousness, and a willingness to be persecuted for the cause of Christ are not exactly your most highly prized values today. But Jesus declared such people to be "blessed"!

Of course one might argue that it's possible to be poor in spirit and hungry for righteousness and the like, while still maintaining a modicum of personal peace. Let me be righteous *alone*, let me be poor in spirit *by myself*, and don't bother me with the dirty laundry of other folk!

I'm sorry, but Jesus won't permit it. Along with the meek and mournful He pronounced a blessing on, of all people, the *merciful*! I don't think that made Him too popular with the crowds back then. Unless I'm completely mistaken, people in the first century were probably just as averse to being concerned with the burdens of others as we are today. Jesus' declaration must have rubbed them the wrong way too.

No one would come right out and say it, but a lot think it: "*Cursed* are the merciful, for they shall be bothered!" A Roman philosopher once called mercy "the disease of the soul"; mercy, like meekness, was considered a sign of cowardice in the ancient world.

Things haven't changed much. People still envy the carefree soul who is a world unto himself, far removed from the entangling complications that others' problems often bring. Many say, "Blessed is he who hasn't a care in the world." "On the contrary," says Jesus, "blessed is he who has a world of cares!" Of course He means the cares of *others*.

If the merciful are blessed, as Jesus says, what becomes of the calloused and uncaring? Are they really free to live in selfish disregard for others, without fear of any adverse consequences? I'll let King David answer that.

Appoint an evil man to oppose him;
    let an accuser stand at his right hand.
When he is tried, let him be found guilty,
    and may his prayers condemn him.

May his days be few;
  may another take his place of leadership.
May his children be fatherless
  and his wife a widow.
May his children be wandering beggars;
  may they be driven from their ruined homes.
May a creditor seize all he has;
  may strangers plunder the fruits of his labor.
May no one extend kindness to him
  or take pity on his fatherless children.
May his descendants be cut off,
  their names blotted out from the next generation.
May the iniquity of his fathers be remembered before
    the LORD;
  may the sin of his mother never be blotted out.
May their sins always remain before the LORD,
  that he may cut off the memory of them from the earth.
    (Psalm 109:6-15)

My goodness! I wouldn't wish that on my own worst enemy. Why should anyone be reckoned worthy of such horrid punishments? Because, says David, "he never thought of doing a kindness, but hounded to death the poor and the needy and the brokenhearted" (verse 16). The King James Version renders it, "Because that he remembered not to show *mercy*."

REASONS FOR OUR RELUCTANCE

So why are we so lax in showing mercy? Why do we withdraw from the burdens of others, rather than hasten to bear them? I have already answered that in several ways, but let me conclude with a few additional comments.

We are often slow to be merciful because we have forgotten how pitiful and wretched we ourselves once were. We have taken God's grace for granted. Forgiveness of our sins has made us forget just how far we had fallen. I'm not suggesting that we wallow in the sinful mud of our pre-Christian past. But our readiness to be merciful in helping others frequently depends on how well we remember how little we ourselves deserve.

Although we were ungodly, unappealing, and unfriendly, God was not put off. Indeed, it was "at just the right time, when we were still powerless, [that] Christ died for the ungodly" (Romans 5:6). It was "in his great mercy" that the Father "has given us new birth into a living hope through the resurrection of Jesus Christ from the dead" (1 Peter 1:3). How then can we possibly be hesitant in showing great mercy to others?

Another obstacle is the mistaken idea that opportunities to be merciful and to bear someone's burdens will simply drop into our laps. One of the worst errors you can make is to sit idly by, waiting for those in need to come to you. You and I must go to them! Passive, laid-back piety may be comfortable, but it rarely helps anyone.

I was especially moved by the story of eleven-year-old Trevor Ferrell, as told by Charles Colson in his book *Kingdoms in Conflict.* It was December 1983, when Trevor saw a television news report on the homeless in Philadelphia. He persuaded his parents to drive him into the inner-city so that he might see it for himself. Near city hall Trevor saw an emaciated man crumpled on the sidewalk. Trevor got out of the car and approached him. "Sir," he said, "here's a blanket for you." Staring at Trevor, he said, "Thank you. God bless you."

That was the first night of many more to come in which Trevor and his parents drove the streets of Philadelphia, trying to help in any way possible. They distributed blankets, clothing, and food as best they could. Others heard of Trevor's activity and became involved. Someone donated a van. That first step of mercy Trevor took one night in December has blossomed into a full-scale ministry involving dozens of volunteers. Said Trevor, "It's Jesus inside of me that makes me want to do this."[2]

The homeless people of Philadelphia didn't come looking for Trevor; he went looking for them.

Third, as a way of excusing ourselves from doing one merciful act, we do another! Only, the "merciful" act we perform is usually much easier and less demanding than the one we avoided. Both deeds are good and righteous and, above all, biblical. But if we can get away with it, we prefer convenient mercy to the sort that gets our hands dirty. So we rationalize not doing the latter by devoting ourselves, where all can see, to the former.

If you haven't guessed it by now, I'm talking about giving money as an act of mercy. All of us have used this excuse. The Bible makes no bones about our responsibility to support the local church with our financial resources. The problem is that it is easy to give our money and then use that as an excuse for not getting more personally involved. Generosity becomes little more than a convenient (and seemingly biblical) way of pacifying a guilty conscience.

When it comes to our attention that someone in the church is hurting or in need, we quickly write out a check and designate it for the benevolence fund. Great! But how often is that done as we silently say to ourselves, "I've done my duty; nothing more is required."

What we must realize is that, while money is always helpful, people need and want *you*. Of course it takes money to put food on the table and a roof over one's head. But of infinitely greater value is your time, your presence, your arms to hold and comfort, your words to encourage and uplift, your tears to sympathize, and your love to console.

Don't let your financial generosity become an excuse for withholding your personal touch. People can usually get by without a lot of possessions, but they will die without other people.

Finally, some Christians are lax in mercy because they have no idea what the Body of Christ, the Church, really is. Bad theology makes for bad ministry. People attend services on Sunday morning and see little more than a gathering of individuals, just so many isolated men and women linked only by the fact that they are there rather than still in bed or on the golf course.

One of the ways in which the Church of the present day differs most from the Church of the New Testament is in our loss of a sense of community and solidarity. For example, consider the word *saint*, which appears some sixty-one times on the pages of the New Testament. Did you know that in sixty of those sixty-one occurrences the word is in the plural: *Saints*? Only once, in Philippians 4:21, is the singular used, and there it is in the phrase "greet *every* saint" (NASB)! The notion of a solitary saint is utterly foreign to the New Testament Church.

Let's look at another important descriptive term for the Christian: *Priest.* Would you be surprised if I told you that there is not a single instance in the New Testament in which a Christian is individually called a priest? Wherever any variation of that Greek word is used to describe believers in Jesus Christ, you will without exception find the plural *priests* or the corporate term *priesthood.*

I'm not in any way denying that you are individually *a* saint, nor am I denying the priesthood of each believer. These are precious truths. I am simply pointing out that in the New Testament the emphasis is on the corporate nature of our existence in the Church.

Think of the various metaphors used to describe the Church: body, people, nation, Kingdom, building, flock. The corporate dimension of religious experience is absolutely integral to the thought of the New Testament. The late David Watson said it best:

> The root of all sin could be called independence; and it is for this reason that God calls us not only into a personal relationship with himself, but at the same time into a corporate relationship with the rest of the people of God. We are to be dependent upon him; and, in the right sense, dependent on one another. In the west we tend to confuse the words "personal" and "private." Certainly our faith is to be a personal faith; but it is not to be private. The New Testament knows nothing of solitary religion.[3]

None of us will ever see ministering in mercy to others, bearing their burdens, for what it is until we see the Christian for what he is. We are not many units, living and working in isolation, but one spiritual organism, members one of another, bonded by the blood of our Lord Jesus Christ and the indwelling Spirit.

MERCY FOR THE MERCIFUL

Let's not end this until we look at both halves of the verse that serves as the title for this chapter. "Blessed are the merciful," said Jesus, "for they will be shown mercy" (Matthew 5:7).

I've done my best thus far not to mislead you about a ministry of mercy. I've been careful to warn you about the personal burdens that invariably come when you seek to bear the burdens of others. Contrary to what you may think, Jesus is not reversing that here.

The promise to the merciful that they shall receive mercy is not a guarantee that fame, fortune, or even token appreciation will follow on the heels of their ministry. When Jesus says the merciful shall themselves receive mercy, we need to ask, "From whom?" and, "When?"

I don't think He means "from other people," not even from those to whom we are merciful. That doesn't mean others will never treat you mercifully in return. It doesn't mean there are no earthly benefits that come to those who bear the burdens of others. Certainly there are . . . occasionally. But the mercy Jesus promises is divine in origin. It isn't the mercy of men He promises, but of God.

It is entirely possible that your efforts to mercifully bear someone's burdens will never reap a reward in this life. They might. But there is no guarantee. The people to whom you lovingly give yourself may never love you in return. Your service for their sake may never be acknowledged, but rudely taken for granted.

But don't despair. God has pledged *Himself* to you. *He* is your exceeding great reward. But when? Never now? Oh yes, sometimes now. But *definitely* later. When our Lord Jesus Christ returns there will be refreshing showers of mercy in which the merciful shall forever bathe.

So, as you apply yourself to the biblical agenda we've set forth, remember this: "God is not unjust; he will not forget your work and the love you have shown him as you have helped his people and continue to help them" (Hebrews 6:10). And remember the prophet's words:

> He has showed you, O man, what is good. And what does the LORD require of you? To act justly and to love mercy and to walk humbly with your God. (Micah 6:8)

What was it that Trevor Ferrell said? "It's Jesus inside me that makes me want to do this." Is Jesus inside you? If He is, . . .

Notes

CHAPTER ONE: A Pastor's Personal Confession

1. Larry Crabb, *Inside Out* (Colorado Springs, Colo.: NavPress, 1988), page 160.

CHAPTER TWO: Barriers to Burden-Bearing

1. This disturbing fact has led some to suggest that Psalm 89 is really a continuation of Psalm 88. But aside from the natural desire to conclude Heman's experience on a higher and happier note, there is little evidence to support this theory.
2. Franz Delitzsch, *Biblical Commentary on the Psalms* (Grand Rapids, Mich.: Eerdmans, 1975), vol. 3, page 23.
3. C. Samuel Storms, *Chosen for Life: An Introductory Guide to the Doctrine of Divine Election* (Grand Rapids, Mich.: Baker, 1987).
4. Gordon MacDonald, *Rebuilding Your Broken World* (Nashville: Oliver-Nelson, 1988), page 25.
5. MacDonald, page 67.
6. MacDonald, page 67.
7. One of the most helpful books I've seen on this topic is Larry Crabb, *Understanding People: Deep Longings for Relationship* (Grand Rapids, Mich.: Zondervan, 1987). I will be referring to this book several times in the pages that follow.

CHAPTER THREE: God Made Us Hungry

1. "P.S. Everyone at This School Hates Me," *The Dallas Morning News*, March 15, 1981, page 8A.
2. Larry Crabb, *Understanding People: Deep Longings for Relationship* (Grand Rapids, Mich.: Zondervan, 1987), page 111.
3. Crabb, page 112.
4. Raymond E. Vath, *Counseling Those with Eating Disorders* (Waco, Tex.: Word, 1986), page 80.
5. Vath, page 80.
6. Vath, page 121.
7. Crabb, page 15.
8. Charles Colson, *Kingdoms in Conflict* (Grand Rapids, Mich.: Morrow and Zondervan, 1987), page 68.
9. Daniel Taylor, "The Fear of Insignificance," *Christianity Today*, February 3, 1989, page 25.

CHAPTER FOUR: But It Sounds So Selfish!

1. John Piper, "Is Self-Love Biblical?" *Christianity Today*, August 12, 1977, page 6.
2. John Piper, *Desiring God: Meditations of a Christian Hedonist* (Portland, Oreg.: Multnomah Press, 1986), page 14.
3. Larry Crabb, *Understanding People: Deep Longings for Relationship* (Grand Rapids, Mich.: Zondervan, 1987), page 109.
4. Crabb, page 108.
5. Piper, page 15.
6. R. C. Sproul, *In Search of Dignity* (Ventura, Calif.: Regal, 1983), page 18.
7. Piper, page 216.
8. C. S. Lewis, *The Weight of Glory and Other Addresses* (Grand Rapids, Mich.: Eerdmans, 1965), pages 1-2.
9. The best available treatment of the issue of sexual abuse is Dan B. Allender's book *The Wounded Heart: Hope for Adult Victims of Childhood Sexual Abuse* (Colorado Springs, Colo.: NavPress, 1990).

CHAPTER FIVE: Do We Blame It All on Sin?

1. Kevin Huggins, *Parenting Adolescents* (Colorado Springs, Colo.: NavPress, 1989).
2. Huggins, page 37.
3. Huggins, pages 117-140.
4. Lawrence J. Crabb, *Effective Biblical Counseling* (Grand Rapids, Mich.: Zondervan, 1977), page 118.
5. See the excellent discussion of this by James Dobson in his book *Hide or Seek*, revised edition (Old Tappan, N.J.: Revell, 1979).

CHAPTER SIX: The Beginnings of Mercy

1. Larry Crabb, *Inside Out* (Colorado Springs, Colo.: NavPress, 1988), page 77.
2. Crabb, *Inside Out*, page 77.
3. Crabb, *Inside Out*, page 120.
4. Larry Crabb, *Understanding People* (Grand Rapids, Mich.: Zondervan, 1987), page 146.
5. Crabb, *Understanding People*, page 139.
6. Crabb, *Understanding People*, page 147.
7. James Dobson, *Hide or Seek*, revised edition (Old Tappan, N.J.: Revell, 1979), page 152.
8. Dobson, page 152.
9. Crabb, *Understanding People*, pages 147-48.

CHAPTER SEVEN: Is Jesus Really Enough?

1. Gerald F. Hawthorne, *Philippians, Word Biblical Commentary* (Waco, Tex.: Word, 1983), pages 198-99.
2. Hawthorne, page 201.
3. J. I. Packer, *Knowing God* (Downers Grove, Ill.: InterVarsity, 1973), pages 245-46.
4. Packer, page 246.
5. Joni Eareckson Tada, *Glorious Intruder* (Portland, Oreg.: Multnomah, 1989), page 249.
6. Tada, page 249.

7. Tada, page 250.
8. Tada, page 251.
9. Max Lucado, *No Wonder They Call Him The Savior* (Portland, Ore.: Multnomah, 1986), page 48.

CHAPTER EIGHT: An Ordinary Man and His Extraordinary Love

1. Lyrics by Alan Jay Lerner, "How to Handle a Woman," *Camelot* (Burbank, Calif.: Warner Brothers Records, Inc., 1965).
2. Kent and Barbara Hughes, *Liberating Ministry From the Success Syndrome* (Wheaton, Ill.: Tyndale, 1987), page 100.
3. Gerald F. Hawthorne, *Philippians, Word Biblical Commentary* (Waco, Tex.: Word, 1983), page 120. Hawthorne and other commentators have drawn attention to the fact that Aphrodite was not only the Greek goddess of love, but also of gamblers. It is said that when the ancients would throw the dice they cried out, "epaphroditus!" literally, "favored by Aphrodite," perhaps hoping that a passionate invocation at the opportune time might improve their luck.
4. C. F. Weigle, "No One Ever Cared for Me Like Jesus," from *Worship His Majesty* (Nashville, Tenn.: Gaither Music Company, Inc.). Copyright Zondervan Music Group.

CHAPTER NINE: Where Never Is Heard a Discouraging Word

1. William L. Shirer, *The Rise and Fall of the Third Reich* (New York: Simon and Schuster, 1960), page 35.
2. See Larry Crabb, *Inside Out* (Colorado Springs, Colo.: NavPress, 1988), page 167.
3. Lawrence J. Crabb, Jr., and Dan B. Allender, *Encouragement: The Key to Caring* (Grand Rapids, Mich.: Zondervan, 1984), page 20.
4. Lawrence J. Crabb, Jr., *The Marriage Builder* (Grand Rapids, Mich.: Zondervan, 1982), page 53.
5. Crabb and Allender, *Encouragement*, page 104.

CHAPTER TEN: Meekness, Rebounds, and Licorice Seeds!

1. Although the Greek word for "humility" (*tapeinos*) is obviously different from that for "meekness" (*prautes*), the spirit entailed by each is sufficiently similar to the other to warrant my treating them as synonymous.
2. Joni Eareckson Tada, *Secret Strength . . . for Those Who Search* (Portland, Oreg.: Multnomah, 1988), page 140.
3. D. Martyn Lloyd-Jones, *Studies in the Sermon on the Mount* (Grand Rapids, Mich.: Eerdmans, 1974), page 65.
4. Quoted by Frederick Dale Bruner, *The Christbook: A Historical/Theological Commentary—Matthew 1-12* (Waco, Tex.: Word Books, 1987), page 212.
5. Quoted in Iain H. Murray, *Jonathan Edwards: A New Biography* (Edinburgh, Scotland: Banner of Truth Trust, 1987), page 322.
6. Quoted in Murray, page 327.
7. Murray, page 329.
8. Murray, page 329.
9. Lawrence J. Crabb, Jr., and Dan B. Allender, *Encouragement: The Key to Caring* (Grand Rapids, Mich.: Zondervan, 1984), page 48.

CHAPTER ELEVEN: God's Second Greatest Gift

1. Jerry Bridges, *The Crisis of Caring: Recovering the Meaning of True Fellowship* (Colorado Springs, Colo.: NavPress, 1985), pages 66-67.
2. John Murray, *The Epistle to the Romans* (Grand Rapids, Mich.: Eerdmans, 1965), vol. 2, page 137.

CHAPTER TWELVE: The Arithmetic of Forgiveness

1. In this as in all biblical parables, elements are included merely for the sake of scenery. Jesus uses details that would have been familiar to His first-century audience, which should not always be pressed for meaning. The "jailers" who "torture" the unforgiving servant are a case in point. Jesus by no means

intends to depict God as cruel, nor does He sanction brutality. If anything is to be drawn from this scene, it is that God will not tolerate a calloused and unforgiving spirit in His children. Divine discipline is always a possibility (cf. Hebrews 12).
2. Jay E. Adams, *From Forgiven to Forgiving* (Wheaton, Ill.: Victor, 1989), page 18.
3. Adams, page 30.
4. Adams, page 63.
5. Adams, page 72.
6. John Calvin, *A Harmony of the Gospels: Matthew, Mark and Luke*, trans. A. W. Morrison (Grand Rapids, Mich.: Eerdmans, 1972), vol. 3, page 170.

CHAPTER THIRTEEN: Mercy in Practice

1. Jackie Pullinger, *Chasing the Dragon* (Ann Arbor, Mich.: Servant, 1980), page 31. I highly recommend that you read two books authored by Jackie Pullinger: *Chasing the Dragon*; and *Crack in the Wall: The Life and Death of Kowloon Walled City* (London: Hodder & Stoughton, 1989).
2. This story is adapted from Peter Lord, *Soul Care* (Grand Rapids, Mich.: Baker, 1990), pages 187-188.

CHAPTER FOURTEEN: "Blessed Are the Merciful"

1. Francis A. Schaeffer, *How Should We Then Live?* (Old Tappan, N.J.: Revell, 1976), page 205.
2. Quoted in Charles Colson, *Kingdoms in Conflict* (Grand Rapids, Mich.: Morrow and Zondervan, 1987), page 256.
3. David Watson, *I Believe in the Church* (Grand Rapids, Mich.: Eerdmans, 1978), page 82.